Henry Edgar

Auguste Comte and the Middle Ages

Henry Edgar

Auguste Comte and the Middle Ages

ISBN/EAN: 9783741134500

Manufactured in Europe, USA, Canada, Australia, Japa

Cover: Foto ©ninafisch / pixelio.de

Manufactured and distributed by brebook publishing software (www.brebook.com)

Henry Edgar

Auguste Comte and the Middle Ages

Auguste Comte

and

The Middle Ages

A LECTURE

GIVEN BEFORE A PRIVATE CIRCLE

IN THE

CITY OF POZSONY

(PRESBOURG)

ON SATURDAY 24 GUTTEMBERG 97

(5 SEPTEMBER 1885)

BY

HENRY EDGER,

In undertaking, a year ago to-day, for the second time, to give a lecture more or less public in this City of Presbourg on the anniversary of the death of AUGUSTE COMTE, the lecture being an exposition of a certain phase of the colossal work accomplished by this great Genius, I felt it necessary to say a few words in explanation of the attitude I presume to take in these Annual Lectures. And if I feel it necessary to do the same again to-day I may congratulate myself that it is for the last time. I am hoping to have ready for the press in the course of this next year a short statement of the general character of the Religion I profess that will render unnecessary similar explanations on any subsequent recurrence of this anniversary.

These Lectures, in fact, in no wise constitute any religious propagande. In them I make no pretention to do any thing more than offer to the intelligent curiosity of the cultivated classes of this city accurate information on a subject with which I happen to be familiar, but which, while very little known among the public, is beginning to attract the attention of the Thinking World all through Europe. The necessity for any such explanation, however, exists no doubt only in my own feelings. Neither the Government of the Country, nor the Clergy, nor the Press, nor even the population or Authorities of the City, can for a moment be imagined to see any ground for concern, or an occasion for any sort of notice, in an occurrence of so insignificant a character as the giving of a lecture in a private room, before an audience convened by personal invitation, and composed only of a handful of persons from among the very exceptional part of the population that is acquainted with the English language. But any thing resembling, *primâ facie*, a religious controversy is so far from being a benefit to a population that it would seem to me a very ungracious act, on the part of a foreigner, to do any thing to bring it about. Not that the noble habits of toleration which have for centuries characterized so admirably the very sympathetic people of this Country — sympathetic both in the English and the French senses of the word — are in the least likely to be at any time found wanting. But it would be an ungrateful return for the generous hospitality a stranger coming hither is sure to experience, to put those noble habits to the test by doing anything that could resemble the introduction of the poisonous apple of religious discord.

The doctrines of the wonderful Genius who bore the name of AUGUSTE COMTE, and who like all geniuses of the very first order, was naturally and inevitably misunderstood altogether by his cotemporaries, especially in his own country, do in fact ultimately result in religion, in a Religious Dogma, that religious dogma being nothing either more or less than the Synthesis of Positive Science regarded as a one whole. On the basis of this dogma will inevitably arise, sooner or later, a Religion, complete in every thing that practically constitutes religion: Worship, Consecration, moral and intellectual Instruction, Culture and Discipline, social and individual Direction and Regulation, Consolation, calming and fortifying under affliction and the inevitable injustice actually characterizing terrestrial existence, with the Prophecy of a Better Future. It would seem, therefore, at first sight, as though lecturés expository of the doctrines of Comte, given, too, by one who is himself an ardent disciple, must necessarily constitute a religious propagande, a propagande tending to introduce a new religion, and with it just that apple of discord alluded to. For certainly no controversies in which men engage are more apt to be bitter and envenomed than those between rival religious creeds; and nothing can be more undesirable for any country, especially one that is in actual enjoyment of religious peace and tranquillity, than to have a war of rival dogmas set up in its midst. But those who have some little acquaintance with Positive Science, even in its lower grades only, mathematical, physical or chemical, will understand, almost at the first glance, even if it could be imagined possible that real religion should ever be based upon a dogma purely scientific, how utterly impossible it must be for a doctrine that is really so, one that is purely scientific, to introduce any such war of rival dogmas. For genuinely positive science never has to spread itself and extend its constantly growing empire over the human mind by popular discussion. Such discussion, indeed, is utterly contrary to its nature. In proportion as really positive science is, in fact, spread among the people, the consciousness of the radical incompetency of popular discussion in the solution of serious questions is spread at the same time; its incompetency, at all events, in the solution of questions in which the intervention of positive science is even conceivably possible. Positive Science trusts for her propagande solely and exclusively to Experience and serious Instruction; that is just why her empire does in fact constantly go on growing irresistibly. The inevitable result of the dissemination of the Positive Doctrine is, therefore, exactly the opposite of that so justly to be deprecated. Instead of tending to agitation it tends irresistibly, wherever it is introduced, in exact proportion to its extension, to social calm. It tends irresistibly to bring into the most profound discredit the whole of the pestilential business of the political, social or religious agitator.

That which specially imposes on the Lecturer the duty of the present explanation is the fact that, in completely private life, in the cases wherein he has had the pleasure of making the personal acquaintance of individuals among the population of this city, he has been unable, as must naturally be the case with any one possessed of deep and fervent convictions, which have proved the source of profoundest consolation, hope and energy to himself, to avoid making efforts to share with his acquaintances the happiness he himself enjoys. Perhaps it were not an unfounded boast to confess that his efforts in this sphere have not been wholly without success. But the Positive Religion of Humanity, arising on the dogmatic foundation of the Scientific Synthesis, imposes upon its adherents, not only the duty of *living for others*, but also and equally that of *living in open day*. Representing Human Life as attaining its just dignity only when the Individual freely and voluntarily consecrates his existence to the social service, it insists upon the absence of all concealment as the only sufficient guarantee of the sincerity and reality of the social consecration. All secret intrigue, all underhand contrivances, everything that ever so little savors of plotting, it calls upon its disciples to utterly eschew, even to abhor; it insists upon their doing all that they do openly and above board, upon their doing nothing, therefore, that is not fully avowable, and upon their fully taking upon themselves the just and proper responsibility of their conduct, be it what it may. Its real adherents can never, therefore, join any secret society, however honorable and avowable the objects of such a Society may be. The condition of secrecy in itself creates a certain presumption of ends and aims to say the least selfish, with a collective if not absolutely individual selfishness, even where not directly anti-social; and, speaking among ourselves, or in addressing disciples, we use upon this point much stronger language.

But the same Religion teaches its adherents also a just respect for the actually existing public opinion, as well as the actually existing social institutions, even in regard to points on which opinion or institutions may be susceptible of rectification. And especially is this due from a Foreigner towards the laws, the institutions, the customs, the manners and all the other social conditions of the country that gives him hospitality. Every thing in the teachings of Comte tends to deeply impress this consideration on the minds of his followers. Especially the representation made by those teachings of the urgent social importance at this day of cultivating the spirit of mutual respect and mutual friendliness between the different nationalities that compose our modern civilization. The beneficent consequences in all regards, moral and intellectual as well as social and political, of such a spirit and temper it were certainly needless to dwell on, or for one moment to urge, for they will be spontaneously felt by every rightly constituted mind; but their only reliable foundation can be in the existence of the same dispositions among the individuals composing these different nationalities, where in fact they do exist in a very remarkable and most encouraging degree already, the ancient sentiments of international hatred, jealousy and dislike being everywhere, at this day confined to limited classes of the populations, classes that have less undergone the reactions of the more wholesome side of the modern spirit.*) And the culture of such a mutual friendliness and respect between the

---

*) The few seeming exceptions to this assertion happily show how ready they are to disappear, as soon as a wiser statesmanship shall arise to set aside the obstacles unwisely or gratuitously placed in the way of the spontaneously developing international amity.

populations themselves, irrespectively of the Governments, is the more important from the fact that the mutual amity friendliness and respect between the different peoples composing our modern occidental civilization, need on every ground to be combined with the political independence of the different nations, independence which, when once all danger of foreign aggression or internal disorder were fully and fairly laid aside, it would be an advantage to develope rather than to further restrict.

The Lecturer cannot help feeling, therefore, that he owes to the public a certain general account of a doctrine that in his private and personal relations he cannot help propagating. He owes it moreover to the few who do in private listen to him to make this more public (although modest and unobtrusive) exposition, exposition that ought finally to receive the further publicity to be given by the press. In fulfilling this duty he is very desirous of avoiding every utterance that could wound the just susceptibilities of any single inhabitant of the city that gives him shelter and protection. The religion that animates his life makes its adherents feel that they have by no means discharged all their duties towards the society, and indeed towards the country, in the bosom of which they live, when they have simply paid their rent and taxes and abstained from any breach of the civil law. Now the name of AUGUSTE COMTE is beginning to become known, throughout the Intellectual World of all Europe, to such a degree as to make an authentic account of the work of his life and of its culminating characteristics a presumable satisfaction of the curiosity, that will naturally have a certain prevalence in this as in any other city equally intelligent. The doctrines of Auguste Comte treat, however, of such subjects, that in giving any sort of account of them one is necessarily treading on delicate ground; and the Lecturer is desirous at the very outset of allaying apprehensions naturally therefore liable to be awakened by the very subjects, apprehensions, however, that are in reality groundless, or the Lecture would certainly not be given. At the same time the subjects do give the greater importance to accurate information in regard to the doctrines of a Thinker evidently destined to be much more widely known than he ever was during his life-time, and one whose very greatness and the vastness of the work he accomplished naturally cause to be in the highest degree misunderstood at the outset, wherever the fame of them may finally reach.

The distinctive characteristic of all the speculations of Comte consists in their fundamental assumption that all phenomena, social and moral phenomena as well as others, are subject to immutable natural law. This assumption does indeed implicitly underlie all distinctively modern thought, and is, too, precisely that characteristic of the actually prevailing opinion, acknowledged or unacknowledged, that is most constantly and most steadily gaining ground. All belief in the supernatural is more and more universally being set down systematically as superstition. It is not therefore the assumption itself that is so much the distinctive and decisive characteristic of the labors of Auguste Comte as its open recognition, and the frank and honest acceptance of all its necessary logical consequences. But the systematic acceptance and open recognition of this underlying principle, at once of Positive Science and of Modern Thought, viz, the universal prevalence of immutable Natural Law, is just that which gives to science a tendency and an ultimate result the very opposite of that which might naturally be supposed, especially as regards its bearings upon religion, as from the very nature of our subject to day we shall forthwith have to very plainly see. It will already be manifest, indeed, that if the hypothesis of the universal prevalence of natural law were to prove in conformity with fact, it would follow that a positive science of Sociology and a positive science of Morals must necessarily exist, if not actually at least potentially.*) Now the Lifework of Comte consisted essentially in founding these two supreme grades of positive science, positive Sociology and positive Morals. This is the same as to say that he actually discovered immutable natural laws at once of social existence and of social development; and also immutable natural laws to which our interior moral existence, at once intellectual and affective, is subject. But if this were really the very fact, every one acquainted with the true force of these terms will see at once, that the fact would be of more tremendous importance than any

---

*) Some speculators in this sphere, with materialistic tendencies and in view of materialistic ends, have proposed to employ the word *Psychology* as the name of the science which treats of individual Human Nature, at the same time inverting its position relatively to sociology.

ever before accomplished on this planet. And an exposition of the doctrines of Comte necessarily consists, therefore, of an exposition of sociological and moral science, of immutable natural laws of Human Existence and Human Development, social and individual; than which a more important subject, at all events, is inconceivable.

It must be observed here, however, that in the process of its development, Positive Science, notwithstanding the undisputed Empire it finally acquires over the human mind, has necessarily to pass through a transitionary hypothetical stage, during which its doctrines have no more authority or influence over the general public, ordinarily indeed much less, than any other sort of doctrine. Only minds of the very rare order that is capable of comprehending, appreciating and verifying directly, the demonstrations on which it rests, are capable at the outset of undergoing its domination and of thus entering into the new Light. For every scientific Discovery, especially one of capital importance, is necessarily at first, even in the mind of the Discoverer himself, only a hypothesis, until he has subjected it to rigorous demonstrations, which are often of so difficult a nature that not a single contemporary can be found to accomplish their verification. The great Kepler declared that he would be himself fully content if he could but be sure that at the end of half a century his works would have found one single appreciative reader. The spiritual allegiance of the general public is always won over by a much simpler and easier, but more indirect, mode of verification, consisting in the fulfilment of the predictions of future occurrences made in the name of the corresponding science. In a word, the hypothetical stage of genuine science terminates for the general public only when the hypothesis has received the decisive stamp of Experience. So much is this the case that, when a new doctrine of any sort, professing to be based upon science, starts at once into a wide popularity, popularity evidently based upon a predilection for the particular doctrines taught, that popularity itself furnishes a pretty strong presumption of a considerable element of charlatanism in that doctrine. For the genuine realities of our existence are by no means apt to be sufficiently flattering to our spontaneously predominant inclinations to secure an immediate welcome: the honest revelation of them is much more often accepted only perforce, and after severe castigations at the hand of that unrelenting Disciplinarian.

A second distinctive characteristic of the labors of Comte, of scarcely less importance than the first, save that without that first it would have remained eternally impossible, consists in the systematic and constant recognition of science as a one whole, a complete and universal Doctrine, the discovery of positive Sociology and positive Moral Science having rendered the empire of science conterminous with the ultimate limits of Human Thought. Indeed the constitution of the Scientific Synthesis, the transformation of science into a one, consistent, fully hierarchical Whole, under the systematic supremacy of sociological and moral science, veritably sacred science, and the substitution of this Synthesis for Specialist science, a heterogeneous assemblage of so-called sciences, separate sciences, with no systematic link between them, no mutual responsibility, so to speak, is the achievement of supreme importance. It was by just this substitution that Auguste Comte changed entirely the relations between Science and R_{eligion}; for specialist science, *whatever the intentions of the savans who cultivate it*, is necessarily materialistic and atheistic in its tendencies; while synthetic science is in all its bearings profoundly religious, sociological and moral science combining to demonstrate that both from the social and the individual point of view, Religion is beyond all comparison man's supreme concern, and that, too, independently of all imaginable dogmatic differences, thus transporting all the influence of Science as a whole from the side of the modern religious indifference, and the materialism and practical atheism on which that indifference is based, to the side of Religion and of Christianity, and therefore to the side of the Churches so far as their purely spiritual action is concerned.

Any one sufficiently acquainted, however, with Positive Science, even in its lower grades or degrees only, mathematical, physical or chemical, will easily understand, and indeed spontaneously see for himself, how impossible it were, in a single lecture, adapted to a popular, even although specially intelligent audience, to give anything like a systematic exposition of either of these two new and supreme grades or degrees of Science, or even of one single phase of either of them, such as is indicated in the announcement of our subject for to-day. An exposition, adapted for instance to a scientific school, even of the Positive Theory of the Middle Ages only, would require various conditions in no wise realizable here to-day. All that is attempted is, to give a general conception of these two new sciences, as they will be called, and which, as being new, remain still, necessarily, in their purely hypothetical stage. To give a conception at once of the scientific synthesis as a whole, and especially of its two supreme degrees, sociological and and moral, sufficiently comprehensive and exact to enable an intelligent mind to judge, whether there be really here something important enough to be worth the trouble of further and more laborious investigation. And above all, such as to enable the statesman and patriot to form an intelligent judgment on the important question, whether the general dissemination of a knowledge of these new and hypothetical sciences, and especially of the new and hypothetical *synthesis of all science*, would be an advantage and clear gain to a nation, or whether it were rather a thing to be watched with suspicion. Dealing with questions so delicate, and of so supreme importance, as the very foundations of religion and morality, it can scarcely help being either the one or the other.

I.

From this point of view, the most important question is, no doubt, the bearing of the scientific synthesis, and of these its two supreme grades, upon Religion. Now the fundamental principle of positive science, universal underlying assumption of all distinctively modern thought, the subjection of all phenomena whatever to immutable natural law, seems at first sight not merely hostile but fatal to religion, as casting profound discredit upon the religious dogma based altogether upon supernaturalist conceptions. But the discredit exists already, inflicted upon the theological philosophy by positive science in general, discredit gradually growing for centuries past, and no doubt at this day being more intensified than ever, and by positive science too. But all this discredit, as actually existing, is necessarily due to specialist science exclusively. The Scientific Synthesis is altogether too new, too little known, so far as known too manifestly hypothetical as yet, to have had, up to this day, any appreciable influence upon public opinion. Positive Science does tend no doubt, positive science in every form, and tend irresistibly, to make all belief in the supernatural be looked upon as superstition. And it does so, not by directly attacking theological dogmas, so much as by constantly furnishing a greater and greater number of purely natural explanations of phenomena formerly accounted for, as indeed was at first the case with all phenomena whatever, on the theological principle; thus giving rise to an irresistible suspicion, that all things have a natural explanation if one could but find it out. And this tendency, again, is much strengthened by the contrast presented between the clearness, the precision, the consistency and the practical utility, as well as the certitude, inherent in scientific conceptions, and the vagueness, obscurity, doubtfulness, and, above all at this day, the moral and practical impotence which characterize the theological or supernatural. It is easy, moreover, to see that this tendency to treat the supernatural as always a mere superstition, sheltering one's self in so doing under the aegis of science, exists in thousands upon thousands of souls that never give themselves the smallest trouble about philosophical speculation or scientific investigation, that would think all those things a waste of time, and one insufferably tedious too, but can still very easily appreciate the convenience of being emancipated from an irksome moral responsibility. The fundamental principle of the Positive or scientific Philosophy, the so-called Law of the Three States, the discovery of which gave birth to sociological science, simply asserts this tendency of modern opinion to be a natural and inevitable one, and to constitute, in fact, at bottom, the fundamental and immutable law of the progress of the human mind.

But, in frankly accepting this tendency as irresistible, and then honestly pushing it on to all its logical consequences, the Scientific Synthesis gets back to Religion, and with a force utterly irresistible. If all supernaturalist explanations of phenomena are to be laid aside, that is simply by means of the substitution of natural explanations. The phenomena to be explained remain unchanged, their reality in no wise diminished by any modifications in our explanations. If Christianity, for instance, Christianity as a great social fact, with all its moral and spiritual splendors, is no longer to be regarded as a supernatural product, then is it a natural product of Humanity, that is to say of the Human Race as a grand whole, working out its normal unity under the immutable natural laws imposed on it in the creation. How can any one, without proclaiming himself incapable of recognizing the moral and spiritual phenomena around him, and those presented by our past history, contrive to evade the cogency of this consideration? It were easy enough, at all events, to go on to the next step, viz. that Christianity, relatively to all the past the supreme product of Humanity, although possibly destined to be absorbed in some still higher development, must necessarily be utterly incapable of simply dying out and disappearing. Dropping indeed its supernaturalism, which, indispensable at the outset, when any other basis for religion would have been inconceivable, has been for several centuries past its one constant source of weakness, and now at last of almost total paralysis, it must necessarily be destined, as to all its fundamental and essential characteristics, as an Ideal of Human Existence, an embodiment of noblest and divinest Human Aspirations, not merely to perpetuation, but to a large development of its efficacy and power.

For religion is one, continuous and eternal; it is only the dogmas that differ and change with the increase and development of the positive knowledge of Mankind. To suppose that Religion, to suppose, therefore, that Christianity, is capable of extinction in any of its grand and sublime characteristics, purely human and purely natural as all these most evidently are, on the theory, that is to say,. of the universality of Natural Law, becomes impossible for any mind with ever so little positive sociological instruction. The human race itself, or at least our modern occidental civilization, were destined rather to perish.

The same thing is true, however, not only of Christianity but of all the so called different religions upon the face of this globe. The dogmas of the past are all alike fictitious. But the religions are all alike real and true. Or to speak more exactly, Religion is one, eternal, indestructible, unchangeable, save only as subject to a progressive, ever higher and higher development. Far, however, from being on a footing of absolute equality, there exist among these Religious Systems of the Past, as among all beings on this Earth of ours, relations strictly hierarchical. All the religious dogmas of the past, and all the different religious systems based upon them, have been indeed perfectly natural developments of the Human Race, all tending towards a Final Unity, truly sublime and glorious, first attempted in the form of Universal Empire, but afterwards in the very much higher form spontaneously indicated by Catholicism, that of a Universal Church, in which form alone it is susceptible of a complete, final realization. The General History of the Human Race, and the History of Religion, the one and the other alike truly told, are in fact one and the same thing. There never has been and there never can be any Human Society that is not based upon Religion, in the scientific, or what is the same thing the universal, sense of the word Religion. In my last year's Lecture[*]) the long, unbroken line of gradual progress was traced from the Fetichistic cradle of the Human Race, up to and including the Great Roman Empire, which laid the most essential foundations of our modern Occidental Society, but still needed certain indispensable conditions that were spontaneously

---

[*]) „Auguste Comte and the Philosophy of History". (Hitherto unpublished).

developed in fact by the Feudo-Catholic Civilization of the Middle-Ages, viz: (1) The double emancipation of the Working Men and of Women, (2) the development of a system of Moral Culture independent of the external, civic life; and closely connected with this, (3) the separation of the Spiritual Power from the Temporal Power. All these merely spontaneous, and therefore provisional, forms of Religion aimed, as did Christianity, at an ideal of moral and social existence, ideal at each successive phase of development carried up to a higher degree of perfection, and attaining under Christianity a veritable sublimity. In this merely spontaneous state, however, no religious system has been capable of maintaining itself indefinitely. In order to be permanent, and effectually carry Human Society forward continuously, and without any further break, towards its true destination, Religion and the Ideal (if indeed they are not absolutely one) must both become systematic, by means of the advent of positive knowledge of the real Laws of Human Nature social and individual. The scientific synthesis, therefore, presents to the adherents of all the religions of the past, the means of attaining with certainty the ends which are common to them all, laying aside nothing but just those divergences, closely linked with the variations in dogmas all alike fictitious, which have struck them all alike with paralysis, but naturally struck with the greatest severity the most advanced.

The impression generally prevailing, wherever there exists only a vague and superficial knowledge of the Positive Doctrine, that this doctrine is atheistic, is equally baseless and erroneous with the idea of its contradicting and being a rival of Christianity. Science, accounting for all phenomena on the principle of immutable natural law, ceases entirely no doubt to recur to the Divine Will as any *explanation* of phenomena. And Specialist Science, occupying itself exclusively with purely material phenomena or with vital phenomena in a purely materialistic spirit, seeking to represent them as identical with the merely chemical and physical, exerts an irresistibly materialistic and atheistic influence, even without any direct contradiction of theological dogmas, influence indeed that does not become in the least degree less energetic, by means of the profession of Christian beliefs, let it be ever so sincere, on the part of the savans who cultivate it. The reading public feels that such a profession is a contradiction; the majority, at least among the more active minds, go farther, and set it down as an insincerity, a prudent and indeed wise hypocrisy, which they will do well to imitate. For this materialistic and atheistic influence depends mainly on the striking contrast before alluded to, between the certainty, clearness, precision and practical utility of scientific conceptions — expression synonymous, so far as the labors of the specialists are concerned, with materialistic conceptions — and the uncertainty, vagueness, inconsistency and growing practical impotence of theological conceptions. And this atheistic influence is very much increased by the efforts of theologians to resist it, seeing that those efforts are obliged, in the absence of the scientific synthesis, to take the form of persistence in claiming the exclusively supernatural basis of Religion and the Church, and the absolute necessity, therefore, for the sake of maintaining these, of maintaining also, however impossible, a belief in the supernatural. The good faith of the savans, the literary and journalistic class, the men of the world, who pretend to accede to this view, may be something more than doubtful. But as soon as ever the Supernatural is laid aside completely and systematically, one can immediately begin to see that if Science, in its religious synthesis, is perfectly silent in regard to the existence of God, and the divine creation of the universe, that silence does not in the smallest degree imply any negation. What the Positive Philosophy*) asserts, in regard to all such questions as those of absolute origins and absolute existence, is simply that they are utterly inaccessible to all our means of positive knowledge, and that therefore the human mind tends, spontaneously and irresistibly, to abandon their discussion in favor of the positive knowledge offered by science. In this it only seconds the theological doctrine itself, which does not pretend to base itself on Science, but on the contrary on Faith. Moreover, the silence of the scientific synthesis is a respectful, a reverential silence. It is simply abstinence from the vain presumption by which finite man, with his so limited powers and capa-

*) The Positive Philosophy is at bottom simply the coordination of the fundamental principles, underlying at once Positive Science itself, and its several logical methods, or rather different degrees of development of a one same method. But, by a legitimate extension of the signification, the term may be employed as synonymous with the Scientific Synthesis itself.

cities, pretends to grasp the Infinite One, and discuss familiarly His transcendent attributes. It is simply the modesty, at once reverential and wise, which, abstaining from the mad ambition that would fain comprehend the Unknowable, grasp the Inconceivable, sound the unfathomable depths, scale the inaccessible heights, resigns itself to the attainment of the knowledge within its reach, and in that wise Resignation receives a vast, a stupendous reward. For experience abundantly proves, now at last, that man's real needs and his means of investigation are strictly correlative. This was long ago proved in regard to the material world. And it is now equally proved, as indeed it would only have been reasonable long ago to have anticipated, in regard to the Spiritual World.

The scientific synthesis is in no wise inconsistent with a profound belief in the Divine Creation of the Universe. For, indeed, as a matter of mere feeling, as an Aspiration, as a „feeling upward" towards the Inaccessible, nothing can be more rational than the Belief that, wherever the limits of positive knowledge may prove to be, there must be a Beyond. Nor can it be very different with the feeling, that when the Being, that is within the sphere of the Knowable supreme, is positively known to us, that *Knowable Supreme* must needs be, relatively to us, *in the direction of the Unknowable Supreme in the Beyond*, and the most perfect Representation of that Absolute Supreme that can by any possibility be even conceivable by us. In this idea there is at all events a ground for Belief in God, far superior in cogency to any that a simply theological Dogma can offer, while here also — and this may be still more important — there is a complete conciliation between the Scientific Synthesis, with its total silence in regard to the creation of the Universe, the Divine Existence, and every thing else in the sphere of the Unknowable, and the most profound, the most devout belief both in the Divine Existence and in the Creation.

The Scientific Synthesis demands, no doubt, a conception of God, and especially of the Relations between God and Man, different from those that have hitherto prevailed; but those which it tends to substitute are infinitely better adapted to inspire adoration, and present the most striking contrast to the semi-contemptuous indifference and scepticism which actually characterize so large a proportion of the nominal Catholics and nominal Christians of to-day. All the modification, in fact, which the scientific synthesis imposes on the belief in God and in the divine creation of the Universe is, that instead of supposing God to have created a disorderly World, so disorderly as to need constant interventions of the divine creative Will, in order to protect His own eternal purposes from defeat by the spontaneous tendencies He had Himself implanted in His creatures, such a belief must recognize that God, whom the Christian Scriptures represent as a Being „in whom there is no variableness nor even the shadow of a turning", did, on the contrary, create a perfectly orderly world, such a world, in fact, and so profoundly orderly, that by virtue of the principles and tendencies implanted in it at the creation itself — principles and tendencies which in their actual operation are revealed to us by positive science under the name of immutable natural laws — it spontaneously works out, without any further intervention, the unchanging purposes of the Infinite Creator. And in thus humbly resigning ourselves to the inevitable fact, that the sphere of Eternal Mystery is boundless, and the sphere of positive Human Knowledge very narrowly circumscribed, not only have we to be penetrated with profound gratitude for the far higher and diviner conception of God thus brought within our reach, and for the general fact, indeed, that pre-eminently in this spiritual sphere are our real needs and our means of acquiring positive knowledge strictly conterminous; but in recognizing the real, the absolute God to be necessarily unknowable, and the completely demonstrable Humanity to be necessarily the highest humanly conceivable Representation of the Divine Existence, and therefore the direct object of our worship, as well as of our supreme affection and our constant and devoted service, we are delivered at one stroke from all the immense, the insurmountable difficulties, moral as well as intellectual, which have always heretofore marred the perfectness of our adoration, and dimmed the brightness of our faith. No human soul can ever completely surmount the terrible moral difficulty involved in the fact, that it is totally impossible really to conceive of an Omnipotent Creator who is not necessarily the Author of all Evil as well as of all Good, until one bows in humble submission before the fact, that the Absolute is necessarily the unknowable, and the Supreme Being whom we can really know, and therefore really worship and love, as well as faithfully serve, must necessarily be only the relatively supreme. This humble and reverent submission once accomplished, nothing can ever afterwards mar the profound and enthusiastic adoration naturally, necessarily inspired by the contemplation of the Ideal Perfection, struggling ever upwards towards a more and more complete realization, under the superincumbent weight of a blind fatality interposing in its path gigantic obstacles. While the same reverent submission delivers us, at the same time, from the violence done, at once to our rationality and our moral sentiment, by the spectacle of a universe needing a perpetual botching and tinkering, to prevent the handiwork of the Creator from defeating the Creator's own designs. The difficulties that have hitherto so profoundly shackled, especially during recent centuries, the energies of Religion, and seem to threaten Her now with definitive extinction, all disappear, and the sublime realities of Christianity, its noble moral and social Ideal intact, only developed to a still higher and diviner level, remain planted on a foundation utterly irrefragable and immovable.

For the scientific synthesis completely demonstrates the absolutely unquestionable validity of all the practical side of Christianity. It sets aside its supernaturalism and that which depends wholly and exclusively upon that supernaturalism. But only most profoundly to confirm, and in fact incorporate into itself, all the rest, all, without suffering one jot or one tittle to pass away unfulfilled.*) And how little indeed is it that thus disappears! How infinitely greater is that which remains, restored in fact by the scientific synthesis, by it picked up out of the mire and mud into which it has been so long trampled by an atheistic and fan-

*) Of course it can hardly be necessary to explain here, what will be spontaneously comprehended by every well regulated mind, that these expressions give not the smallest countenance to the pretensions of the unauthorized and incompetent to hang their own crude schemes upon the literal expressions of the New Testament, or any other Text whatsoever. Modern society will certainly not go back, for instance, to the Communism of the Early Christians, or any other form of anarchical Equalitarianism, alike chimerical and degrading, and degrading most of all to the popular mass. Besides, it is the scientific synthesis that is the supreme Authority as to the question, what it is that constitutes Christianity, as Religion, when the theological dogma is laid aside. Only it is certainly not the *omissions* that will ever shock, or be complained of by, any Christian whomsoever, be he ever so fervent, devout and self sacrificing.

fastical philosophy, a materialistic science and a still more materialistic and atheistic Industrialism, which, in its actual unregulation, individualism and anarchy, is no progress at all, but only a hideous, infernal monster devouring its own children. There is no progress at all, but only an unspeakable degradation, something far lower down than any mere retrogression, in the setting up as the Ideal, the real and practical Ideal of men, and even of women too, the veritable object of worship and service for at least six days out of the seven, and with a constantly growing tendency to include all the seven, to make even the temple services themselves subordinate to this really dominant ideal, the Sardanapalian Ideal — the Getting, the Having and the Enjoying of material objects and selfish gratifications. The scientific synthesis decisively demonstrates, that the grand spiritual realities of human nature, and especially that which has been so admirably treated of by the Catholic Mystics as the Interior Life, and the sublime social and moral destinies of the human race revealed by christianity, and so grandly and nobly worked out by the Christian Church in the past, especially by the eternally venerable Catholic Church of the Middle Ages, that truly heroic period of religion and morality, are none of them dependent in the smallest degree upon the theological dogmas with which they were historically linked, and ten centuries ago, in fact, necessarily linked. The theological dogmas may utterly disappear, but all this other side of Christianity, the really and eternally grand, sublime, truly divine side, will remain intact, not a jot nor a tittle of the spirit of it being disturbed or compromised in the smallest degree, this „spirit that giveth life" being protected the rather against any further possibility of being sacrificed to „the letter that killeth". Christianity, in fact, in all that practically constitutes its essential elements, is only confirmed, placed on the immovable, irrefragable basis of positive demonstration, carried up moreover to yet higher flights of sublimity. All this higher side of christianity, all the very essence of the Christian Religion remains, as the Eternal Aspiration of our race, gradually developed athwart the centuries, by the ministry of the highest and most exquisite individual products of that race. It remains as the undying Ideal of the race, yes, and its predestined end too. In spite of all the grovelling tendencies which so strikingly mark the passing hour, Mankind will still go on struggling upward towards the ideal gradually developed by our race, and which ideal, constituting the essential characteristic of human nature, evidently has for its true name Humanity, seeing that it is it which differentiates that human nature from mere brute nature, from that merely animal and vegetative life which the dominant philosophy would fain represent, with the addition simply of a beaver-vulpine intellect, as the whole of our human nature. And the scientific synthesis comes now, therefore, not merely to furnish a dogmatic foundation that nothing can ever in the smallest degree shake, on which the Culture of the Ideal may be gradually re-instituted, in proportion as the old theological dogmatic basis fails it — and the theological dogma does in fact abandon the moral ideal to a far greater degree even than it is itself openly abandoned by cotemporary opinion — but it comes also to render to the ideal and its culture, in other words to religion, a yet further service, capable of becoming far more immediately effective and energetic. It comes, in fact to make it possible for the theological dogmas, or rather for the theological churches, so far as they yet retain any hold at all upon the modern mind, to consecrate themselves once more to the energetic service of the noble Christian Ideal, the admirable christian moral type, and thereby regain, as most unquestionably, in following so dignified a policy they could not fail to do, a very large measure of their ancient social prestige and glory, and even of their purely spiritual power.

For the Scientific Synthesis entirely sustains Christianity in its general representation of human nature as needing a profound regeneration, and of the true destiny of man as consisting in the eternally progressive consecration of his merely exterior existence to the culture and development of a noble interior existence, under the guiding influence of an ideal of moral and spiritual perfection, which becomes only the higher and diviner for being referred directly to Humanity; under the reactions of which interior life he has, on pain of forfeiting his true destiny and sinking into a degradation which has no name, to more and more subordinate, in his practical life also, his egotist and animal instincts, the lower side of his nature, to the social sympathies and disinterested impulsions, to that Universal Love which the Christian Scriptures declare to be essentially identical with the Divine Nature itself.*) In all this it manifestly presents a marked, indeed glaring contrast to specialist science, and other doctrines claiming at this day a more or less scientific character, and pursuing, or at least tending towards, the same general end as specialist science, viz, the materialistic degradation of our human kind. But in proportion as Auguste Comte advanced towards the complete systematization of the scientific synthesis, furnishing thus to religion a dogma incomparably superior to any she had been able before to attain, he, at the same time, and by the same operation, more and more clearly demonstrated the exact nature of the distinction between Dogma and Religion, and the imperative necessity of subordinating in practice the Dogma, which is but a means, to the Religion, which is the supreme and indispensable end. It was naturally a hard lesson to teach to neophytes, enraptured with the possession of a system combining the highest conceivable sublimity in the doctrines, with a granitic solidity in the foundations. It was a great

---

*) „God is Love." 1 John IV. 8.

misfortune that a premature death took him
away from us, before he had had time sufficiently
to impress upon his disciples the necessity, if
they would be fully consistent with the whole
of the teachings of moral and sociological science,
of systematically subordinating dogmatic instruction to the development of religious practices.
This, however, will be the distinctive characteristic of the grand movement of religious reconstruction, and social and moral regeneration,
that will necessarily spring up, sooner or later,
on the basis presented to religion by the scientific synthesis. The positivist Religious Propagande will bear no resemblance whatever to
the formation of a new sect in the bosom of
our modern society, or employ any of the
methods one would expect on the part of a
new religion. The positive religion of Humanity is not, properly speaking, a new religion.
Sociological science has demonstrated that
religion is essentially one. For religion
is, at bottom, the systematic development of
the Human Unity, social and individual. Let
theological beliefs disappear totally, that Culture of the Human Unity, which has in fact
grown up spontaneously under their ægis, will

have lost not one tittle of its importance. It will remain in the future, what it has been in the past, the indispensable foundation of Human Existence, both social and individual. The actual revolutionary state on one side, of which state temporal repression serves only to increase the intensity, and on the other side the constant and progressive increase of nervous disorders, insanity and suicide, concurrently with the immense improvement of sanitary conditions, so far as regards those merely physical and chemical, are more than abundantly sufficient demonstration of this fact. Refusing *the name* of Religion to that culture, which all the so-called religions of the past actually did furnish, but which theo logical religions have become powerless to maintain, their forces being absorbed in the fruitless struggle to maintain a belief in their dogmas, makes no difference whatever to the fact of the indispensable necessity of this systematic culture of the social and individual unity, which, whether called religion or not, is equally man's supreme necessity.*) And for this culture the scientific syn-

*) When it is considered that in this sense the word „unity" is synonymous with „sanity" (in the fully integral sense of this latter word), the undeniable character of the assertion in the text becomes manifest.

thesis demonstrably furnishes incomparably the most perfect dogmatic foundation imaginable.

Now the energy of religion, as such a culture, resides in its practices, above all in its Worship. Simply making the Positive Dogma the basis of the system of Public Instruction, would in no wise suffice to terminate the modern anarchy and disorder, even if it were possible, which it certainly is not, in the absence of the corresponding religion. But the only Religious Practices based wholly on the scientific synthesis which are not at this day premature, are the purely personal; and the positivist religious propagande will, therefore, necessarily aim especially, and at first almost exclusively, at the dissemination of the practice of the purely personal positive prayer, and address itself by preference, therefore, to the isolated individual. For it is evidently only the purely personal practices that can sufficiently prepare for any collective adorations; while these again can in the first instance be only purely domestic. It is only after a long preparation in these more restricted spheres, the purely personal and the domestic, that the grand and sublime Festivals of the fully Public Worship of Humanity can be practically inaugurated, and that only in a social situation spontaneously prepared for it by that evolution in opinion, from Theology towards Positive Science, which is going on everywhere throughout our modern European society, and producing, as long as the evolution remains purely spontaneous, and therefore necessarily irreligious, more and more profound social disorders, disorders which in fact nothing but the inauguration of the Public Worship of Humanity can ever definitively terminate.

Meantime the Positivist School, simply as a School of Science and Philosophy, pursues its calm, quiet, dignified but unobtrusive action upon public opinion, action becoming gradually irresistible, by virtue of the profound harmony between its teachings and the spontaneous and immutable tendencies of modern Thought. It may be permitted to the Lecturer to remark here, incidentally, the striking contrast presented by the action of this school to that of the partisans of other modern doctrines, substituting as it does a calm, patient, unobtrusive public instruction, for the noisy discussions and popular agitations by which our modern society is harassed and fatigued, in the interest of all sorts of doctrines and schemes each of which would fain impose itself by force, and violence upon a reluctant public.

But still, however certain the ultimate triumph and universal prevalence of the scientific synthesis may be, Auguste Comte saw finally, that the object and aim which constituted the supreme, all-mastering passion of his life, the definitive surmounting of the modern anarchy and disorder, needed yet another and more decisive line of action, on the part of his more unhesitating and radically faithful followers. While he had fully demonstrated that the Social Inauguration of the Systematic Worship of Humanity, is the only possible means of definitively terminating the actually existing and ever-growing revolutionary agitation, the task of accomplishing this Inauguration is one which may very possibly occupy at least whole generations yet to come, although perfectly certain to be accomplished sooner or later. The question therefore necessarily arose, the question moreover of incomparably the most pressing and immediate importance: what can be done in the meantime to arrest the progress of this revolutionary agitation, and prevent the terrible conflagrations with which it threatens our modern society. Auguste Comte, in this situation, so full of dangers, strongly urged upon his disciples the duty of employing the scientific synthesis, first and foremost, as a means of enabling the actual churches to regain much of the social prestige and purely spiritual power of which they have been quite wrongly, irrationally and altogether empirically deprived. It is only ignorance — sociological ignorance — on the part of the public, that makes it attribute to the religion and the moral ideal of christianity, the discredit at this day inevitably attaching to its dogma. There is not the smallest shadow of any justification, furnished by science as a whole, for the actually prevailing religious scepticism and indifference. It is this prevailing religious indifference that is the source whence is being distilled the spiritual dynamite, that threatens one day to explode, no one can tell how soon, and strew all Europe with ruins. It was therefore the duty of his disciples, those at all events who aspired to carry on the great religious work, for which the scientific synthesis furnished the dogmatic foundation, to take their stand between the christian churches on one side, and atheistic and materialistic science, in a word specialist science, and the metaphysical philosophy in all its forms, on the other side, and, in the name of synthetic science and positive philosophy, to defend the cause of a sound spirituality, the Cause of Religion, the cause of Christianity, the cause of the Churches themselves, therefore, so far as regards all their purely spiritual interests, and so to make it possible for them to resume their old attitude of spiritual and moral energy, whereby they would inevitably regain very much of their long-lost social prestige, and so be able, by bracing up the general moral tone, and infusing some little beginning at least of moral regulation into our practical and industrial life, to rescue our modern civilization from the imminent dangers which threaten it. It is mainly the fact that, by the decay of theological religion, our industrial life is given over at this day to utter materialism and practical atheism, in other words to a state of total moral anarchy and unregulation, that has exposed modern society to its present dangers. And it is very plain that, in the actual state of public opinion, the Temporal Government is totally powerless to deal effectually with our modern Industrial Life, its attempted interference, indeed, running serious risk of increasing the actual evils. The theological churches, whose dogma is adapted only to an essentially military society, are totally incompetent alone to regulate a society become radically industrial: Positive Sociology and Positive Moral Science are indispensable guides in an operation so difficult and so delicate: but, resuming their ancient function, in the Middle Ages so admirably sustained, of the culture of the human heart, the development of noble sentiments of devotedness and universal love, the systematic prevalence of which can alone give a real dignity to Human Individual Existence, while alone furnishing a secure foundation for the Social Harmony, they could not fail to experience a very large measure of rehabilitation in public opinion, seeing that in all that supremely important element of the christian doctrine, which ought to be regarded as its true, its highest end, it has now positive science fully on its side, reaffirming, on just those logical foundations which experience has proved to be irrefragable, all its fundamental assertions. The supernatural element in the theological dogma inevitably remains under its actual discredit; but still with this difference, that while the scientific synthesis recognizes the impossibility of any systematic assertion in the sphere of the absolute, it protects even this element of the theological doctrine from systematic denial. In the very act of transforming positive science into religious dogma, the scientific synthesis proclaims unhesitatingly, and in unmistakeable terms, the necessary supremacy of religion, irrespectively of all dogmatic differences, as the only basis on which Human Society can by any possibility ever rest. It paves the way thus for a **Universal League of Religion**, in which all the different Christian Churches, not to speak of other Religions, may, on the common basis of the separation of the spiritual power from the temporal power, but without any compromising formal compact on the part of any one of those Churches, and simply by tacitly abstaining from sacrificing their Religion to their Dogma, present an essentially united front to the common Enemy, the hydra-headed enemy, whose general name is **Irreligion**, among whose many heads we see the hideous forms of Vice, Sensualism, Selfishness, Disorder, Revolt, Despotism, Anarchy. Positive Science in fact, after having so long been the enemy of religion, becomes henceforth its faithful servant. No doctrine can henceforth, pretending to be positive science, fail in this condition, without stamping upon its own brow the indelible brand of Charlatanism. But the abject slave of religion, no, by no means: that were an infidelity to its high calling. To pretend to treat that as true which is known not to be true; to pretend to treat that as certain which is known to be beyond our means of rational investigation — that on the part of science, or its systematic organs, were a treason to the cause of religion itself, perpetuating the sway of Scepticism. Doubt and Uncertainty in this sphere, now that the possibility is fully demonstrated, of putting an end for ever to those so fatal sources of the weakness, and indeed of the very paralysis of religion, which to-day we have so profoundly to deplore. And it is to bring out into its legitimate prominence this side of the actual situation, and of the part to be played in it by the Positive Religion of Humanity, and especially in the Development of the Universal League of Religion, that the Lecturer is writing the little work before alluded to.*)

What has been during the present century called Philosophical History, places itself tacitly at just the same point of view as Positive

*) „Simple and summary Indications concerning the Positive Religion of Humanity."

Sociology. It studies social phenomena as the natural products of their antecedents, and as tending naturally to bring about their consequences. It does so however only tacitly and not systematically, in order to avoid an open and direct contradiction of the theological dogma, side by side with which it has to contrive to subsist, as part of the same official system of public instruction. None the less does this same Philosophical History treat religion as, in its purview, simply a social phenomenon, a purely natural phenomenon. Its professors may be ever so much nominally christians, but none the less is the influence of their teachings upon theological beliefs the same as that of the scientific specialists, except that the materialistic and atheistic tendency is still more pronounced and decisive. It institutes for the intellectually cultured classes, and indeed for the reading public generally, a complete personal emancipation from the very last trace of any real belief, either in theological dogmas or in the religion based upon them, generally combined, it is true, with an external profession of the officially prevailing religion, be it what it may, and with just sufficient external conformity to its practices to avoid any open appearance of rupture. Such a conformity, in itself wise no doubt, is intended to aid in imposing on the less instructed, assumed to be in greater need of the restraints of religion, and on the lower classes, so manifestly in greater need of its consolations, a belief in the only doctrines generally regarded as capable of furnishing to religion its indispensable dogmatic foundation. The motive is excellent, and indeed worthy of all praise; and certainly the churches, the catholic church especially, cannot be blamed for not having refused such a support and repudiated so influential an adhesion, however manifestly insincere. But the catholic church has never been really blind to the great and growing dangers of such a situation, least of all that eminent body which at this day constitutes its supreme and most vital force. It was simply impossible to change that situation. The Church had neither fulcrum nor lever. Men's real beliefs were no longer on its side. Not a single Government in Europe was any longer willing to lend it the aid of the temporal arm; and, besides, a most decisive experience had shown the impotence of the temporal arm, in our occidental civilization, to accomplish anything in the spiritual sphere beyond the intensification of its disorder. However excellent the motive and intention, the method of the specialist savans and of the philosophical historians, was, from its very first inception, in spite of the warm and almost enthusiastic reception it met with in the great world, doomed to inevitable failure, if only by one radical and fatal vice, viz: that of being in direct opposition to the fundamental tendencies of Human Nature. The scheme overlooked two or three of the principal facts in the case, oversight rather singular on the part of savans and philosophers, who pride themselves especially on the strictest fidelity to natural realities, on being indeed above the reach of human delusions. It overlooked these three facts among others: (1) That it is men's real beliefs that are apt to control their actual life; (2) that inferiors are very apt to imitate their betters, especially in following the bent of their spontaneous inclinations; (3) that information of all kinds tends to spread itself more rapidly than ever at this day, when a certain degree of education, just enough at all events to be dangerous, is being every where popularized, the temporal governments themselves aiding. It is hard to today a rural nook sufficiently remote from Railroads, Telegraphs and Newspapers not to furnish peasants, who may be heard saying to each other over their cups: „Our Masters want us to believe in God, but they don't believe in Him themselves". And unhappily there are only too many demagogical agitators ready to exploit the dangers necessarily involved in such a situation.

Now it is by openly and systematically recognizing the subordination of social and moral phenomena to immutable natural law, that Dynamic Sociology completely demonstrates the unimpeachable validity of all that there is left in Christianity when the supernatural element is dropped out. To stop just now to add any further and more detailed demonstrations of this fact would take too long, and besides it would be going beyond the limits imposed, by many and various considerations, on these Lectures. The question belongs rather, so far as any further demonstration may be needed, to the little work above spoken of.

But by pretending to accept absolutely the officially prevailing religion, to submit absolutely to the officially established churches, and swallow whole and entire their theological dogma, which dogma their own works render totally incredible to any man of common sense who really gives credence to those works, the Specialist Savans and Philosophical Historians create precisely the most dangerous elements of all in the actual situation. They do now what the casuists did formerly, only for a different and now very much wider class. They institute, for the reading world, a combination between a merely external and perfunctory adhesion, which no longer deceives any body, and a profound, only half concealed scepticism relative, not merely to the theological scaffolding of Christianity, but to all its sublime moral and social Ideal, to that same sublime social and moral Ideal of which sociological Science, on the contrary, demonstrates irrefragably the essential reality and unimpeachable validity. That merely external adhesion served a valuable, and indeed indispensably necessary, purpose two or three centuries ago, even down to, if not long after, the days of the *Lettres provinciales*, notwithstanding that the eminent Author of these, dreaming of a veritable resuscitation of Theology, was naturally blind to the fact; but at this day it works most fatal mischief, weakening the Church instead of strengthening Her, nay utterly paralyzing Her for any effective moral regulation, even of Her own sincere adherents, and so creating the fatal indifference to religion which every where characterizes our modern civilization, preparing for it the most fatal catastrophes.

II.

The exposition now completed of the relations betwen the Positive Doctrine and Religion, is by no means simply prefatory to the special subject of to-day's lecture, but is, on the contrary, a principal element in its exposition. Without it, it would be impossible to understand the positive theory of the Middle Ages, or, in fact, any theory in the smallest degree scientific in regard to this most interesting, but miserably ill-understood, period. For, instead of having been a period of darkness, and its civilization, as compared with the Greco-Roman, a retrogression, the Middle Ages did in fact realize for mankind the greatest and most sublime progress ever achieved.

The principal source of the false notions that have hitherto prevailed, in regard to this most decisive period of past history, consists in the total absence of any rational and consistent conception of what it is that constitutes Human Progress, and of the supremely decisive relations subsisting between social progress proper and moral progress. The scientific synthesis alone makes clear what it is that constitutes progress, both the social and the moral; and what is still more important, the real relations between Progress and Order. In the two sentences just pronounced, the word „order" might be substituted for the word „progress" (and in the last phrase the two words transposed) without any serious change in the meaning. For it is now demonstrated, that the only real and true progress is that which consists in the development of the Normal Order. While the one eternal moral problem of our Race, has been the subordination of the spontaneously predominant Egotism in our nature, to the Altruism whose prevalence is indispensable to our personal unity, its one eternal social aspiration has been its own Unity, end towards which it has constantly, amidst gigantic obstacles, slowly but surely advanced.

In order to see clearly how very far the Middle Ages carried us along this double road, which is essentially one, for the moral unity and the social unity are at bottom but two different phases of a one same phenomenon, we must keep constantly in view the two elements, the spiritual and the temporal, of which this decisive period was composed. Catholicism on the one side, and on the other side Feudalism, built up a social system which, while incapable of endurance under the then inevitable conditions, incapable therefore of yielding its natural practical fruits, did still, in its essential and fundamental principles, approach incomparably nearer to the Normal State of Human Existence, state alluded to in the Christian Scriptures as the Kingdom of God upon the Earth, than any thing developed, nay anything barely imagined previously. In fact it was the spectacle presented to modern Thought by the Middle Ages, that alone rendered possible the positive Discovery of the Future state of Man upon the Earth. For with a sufficiently relative method of examination, and due allowance for the then unavoidable and insurmountable hindering conditions on the one hand, and for the modifications to be rendered inevitable by the subsequent acquisitions of positive knowledge, the Middle Ages present us with a complete Synthesis of Human Aspirations. All that the Human Race, by its greatest sages, had dreamed of and longed for as supremely desirable, all that Man has constantly struggled for, and fought for, and cheerfully gone through terrible sufferings to finally insure for his Kind, were all at last in the Middle Ages attained, at least in germ and in fundamental principle, but at every point needing for the full realization of the just and necessary practical results, certain conditions not then attainable, conditions which have become attainable only now, or rather, to speak more exactly, in the very near if not absolutely immediate Future; yet of course not even then, or indeed at any time attainable without due effort, perhaps even heroic effort. Such blessings as we enjoy today cost our Forefathers very heroic effort: if we are no longer capable of such effort, our children must wait for their inheritance, ripe though it be in so many respects, until a nobler generation arise to achieve it.

The fundamental feature of Feudalism, stripped of technicalities, of merely temporary accidents of the situation and merely transitional characteristics, was the conciliation between concurrence and independence. The local chiefs had a large measure of independence, and yet the common action, necessary for defence of the general interests, was assured by a hierarchical subordination, stretching downwards from the monarch all the way to the lowest ranks, who now, for the first time, advanced from actual slavery to serfage, and then finally to the essential freedom, in which the necessary social convergence was, as in the case of the ranks above, represented by specific services, defined with sufficient strictness, as due to the immediate superior. This was the natural result of the grand Roman development, entirely irrespectively of the inroads of barbarians, result of that spontaneous transformation of the social activity, from a state of conquest to one of defence, which had been accomplished, or at least prepared for, by the Roman Empire. The development was purely spontaneous however. The profoundest thinker of that age could not have formally expressed in words the grand social phenomenon then being actually accomplished around him. He could not even form in his own mind any sort of conception of it save the most vague and general. It was only the Roman Poet (with that astonishing intuitive insight and foresight, long ago observed as characterizing the true poet, but only now explained by positive moral science) who had indicated the veritable destination of the Roman arms, „*to impose upon Man by War the arts of Peace*".*) But it is only at

*) One hears at this day all sorts of talk, and boastings *ad nauseam*, about **Progress**: but is not this a rathei strange „progress?" Twenty centuries ago, *before the advent of Christianity even*, men could recognize the destination of war as purely transitional, being no other in fact than to render possible the institution of permanent and universal peace. But now, after all our „progress", war is, if certain current theories are valid, to be eternized by having for its function the extension of the commerce of „the Strong" peoples to the disadvantage of the Weak; disadvantage which includes (according to an unvarying experience) their slow death and ultimate extermination, sole definitive result hitherto, of all permanent contact between our Occidental Civilization, in its actual state of anarchy and demoralization, and any of the Backward Races still subsisting on this Globe. As a highly natural and indeed inevitable correlative of such a „Progress", all the principles of Christianity, and indeed of morality in any shape, are openly defied, relatively to the collective (or political) action of mankind, either systematically declared inapplicable, or treated with contempt as „sentimentalism". Meantime a wretched Quackery, that with cynical insolence dares usurp the sacred name of Science, starts up, ready to justify this modern mode of unmitigated cannibalism, blasphemously dubbing it „Evolution!" And the Christian Churches stand by, shutting their eyes and this day, and only by those initiated into the Positive Doctrine, that the full significance of the fact thus, as though by inspiration, revealed, can be fairly appreciated. For even now, now that the light of sociological science has actually come, the great majority of minds will fail to realize the social transformation, in which they are themselves unconsciously taking part.

In the Middle Ages, Industry had not by any means actually replaced War, as the ultimately definitive form of the social activity. It needed all the five centuries of the gradual decay of the mediæval system, and the concurrent gradual development of Modern Society, in order to the accomplishment of this most decisive step towards the coming of the Kingdom of God, in scientific Language the systematic reign of Humanity, upon the Earth But even then this final and definitive transformation of the social activity, proved not to be possible without a severe Crisis, which is not yet by

stopping their ears, or, when sufficiently dominated by the Plutocracy, make themselves active accomplices. This condition of things it is, before all others, which must be modified, and that right speedily, unless Modern Society, in being utterly torn to pieces by revolutionary forces, is to meet a justly deserved fate.

any means terminated, but in the midst of which we are still living. The transformation, however, of military activity, from a state of Conquest to a state of Defence, was a most important and indeed indispensable transition; and this transition was virtually, although only spontaneously, accomplished by the Middle Ages. Until, however, this transition, from being merely spontaneous becomes systematic, by the complete social prevalence of the corresponding theory, the chief benefits destined to flow from that great transformation are profoundly compromised. For aggressive wars, even within the nominal Christendom, remain still possible, although ever more and more costly, ever inflicting more and more cruel sufferings upon the nations, victors and vanquished alike. They are simply struck with radical and incurable sterility, and ever more and more so, their results having, within our occidental civilization, no reliable permanence whatever, save only in the cases where those results might have been better attained without any war at all. Such wars, within the limits of that modern European or Occidental Civilization, have more and more the peculiarly malignant character which marks civil wars: they are more and more disorderly and revolutionary in their essential character, and add, more than any thing else in the purely temporal sphere, to the revolutionary agitation already so dangerously characterizing our modern society.

But the Feudo-catholic civilization, could fully effectuate only in general principle the transformation of conquest into defence, and in no wise assure all the advantages ultimately to be derived from the conciliation between personal independence and social concurrence, which was essentially involved in its temporal system, advantages necessarily reserved for the Normal State of Man upon the Earth, state which, amidst so gigantic obstacles, is now spontaneously working itself out, and as regards the final result irresistibly so. Feudalism introduced, however, especially by its supreme efflorescence, the incomparable Institution of Chivalry, an immense amelioration in the relations between Superiors and Inferiors, an amelioration immeasurably greater than had ever been dreamed of by the most daring of Greek philosophical and social speculators, and in comparison with which the subversive schemes of modern socialists are simply contemptible. It was purely to Feudalism that we owe the fundamental conception, on which the normal social order essentially reposes, so far as the purely temporal order is concerned viz: that *Allegiance and Protection are reciprocal*, principle that, with all the modern anarchy and disorder, no one has dared openly to gainsay; it is simply rendered inefficacious, in the most important cases practically null, by the absence of any effective spiritual power, with a dogma in any wise applicable to a systematically industrial society. But it was Chivalry, and the admirable moral development due to the Worship of the Virgin Mother, which Chivalry, more even than Catholicism itself so much shackled in its noblest inspirations as this latter is by its dogma, admirably cultivated and developed, and by which in its turn it was itself so much ennobled — it was Chivalry that imparted to this principle its highest perfection, and without being able to formulate the maxim by which the scientific synthesis characterizes this class of social relations, did still better, by furnishing practical illustrations which suggested that maxim to the Great Thinker: *Devotedness of the Strong to the Weak, veneration of the Weak for the Strong.*

The complete realization, however, of the normal conciliation between independence and concurrence can be due only to that other condition, which the mediæval civilization has the eternal honor of having spontaneously revealed to Man: *the complete separation and radical independence of the two powers spiritual and temporal.* It is only under the ægis of a Universal Church, fully representing public opinion, that vast, that immense force which, even at this day, wholly deprived as it is of any organ in the least degree worthy of it, manifests so plainly its tendency to become finally every where supreme, — that it will be possible, and fully consistent with a national independence secure against external attack, to develope the local autonomy sufficiently to satisfy the modern aspirations towards freedom, or permit (at bottom essentially the same thing) the definitive abandonment of the whole governmental system of militarism. But, on the one hand, a theological dogma is, in practice, irreconcilable with the effective separation of the two powers, notwithstanding the text of the new Testament that seem expressly designed to furnish a dogmatic basis for it, and notwithstanding also the indisputable fact that the mediæval Church first gave to the world an actual example of a spiritual power independent of all the various temporal governments, and yet uniting into a one spiritual Family, with a sufficient cohesion to be a complete defence against external attack, and also with a universally respected Umpire in interior international difficulties, a considerable number of peoples entirely independent of each other nationally and politically.

But a theological dogma necessarily pushes a Church that is based upon it, even in spite of the essential spirit of the corresponding Religion (which is far from being absolutely identical, or even necessarily in close harmony, with its dogma) towards a theocratic usurpation, as soon as ever it has sufficiently undisputed prevalence to make such a usurpation possible. It is not in the nature of things, that a priesthood, professing to speak in the name of an omnipotent God, a God, moreover, supposed to interfere directly, by supernatural and therefore inscrutable means, in the affairs of men, should limit itself strictly to offering counsels, when command is in anywise within its grasp. And moreover to offering counsels which, whether public or private, are to remain fully liable to rejection by those to whom they are addressed, a rejection entirely at their own option and on their own sole responsibility, responsibility limited exclusively to the inevitable acceptance of the purely natural consequences following such a rejection, and also, in fact, to such consequences as may result from the direct or supernatural intervention of God Himself. Such a limitation is, of course, the practical result of the honest and sincere separation of the two powers, which is not only the fundamental and indispensable condition at this day of all highly developed social order, but the still more inseparable condition of all profound moralization, incomparably the most pressing need of our modern occidental civilization. It is a sheer impossibility that any body of men, professing to speak in the name of such a God should abstain from using Command instead of limiting themselves purely to Counsel, when command has become possible for them, and they have thus behind them an omnipotent God, ready to back up their commands by a direct interference with the natural order, and thus to completely crush any attempt at resistance. It is quite impossible that a Priesthood, speaking in the name of a God of inscrutable purposes, who is the immediate superior alike of Pope and of King, should even imagine the possible existence of any obstacle to the employment of of temporal weapons in the enforcement of the Divine Commands, whenever it can in fact by any means procure the use of those weapons for any such purpose. Nay, such an enforcement must needs seem the duty of the Temporal Government.

And even when the direct interference of the Divine Omnipotence in human affairs, by supernatural means, comes to be pretty generally regarded as essentially fabulous, so generally indeed that the priesthood itself cannot help at least half suspecting that such an appreciation is in accordance with realities, it cannot be in any wise an easy matter for a Priesthood, long habituated to the attitude of command, not only natural but essentially inevitable where there is a real and profound belief in the theological theory of Divine Government, to abandon definitively all direct or indirect recourse to temporal or material weapons, and limit itself exclusively to purely spiritual instrumentalities, instrumentalities moral in the double sense of the term. The Catholic Church is entitled to very much more consideration than she has received, even in the most Catholic countries of our modern Europe, at the hands of the statesmen. Especially seeing that the only policy they have thus far been able to oppose to the theocratic pretentions of that Church is the pure retrogression involved in a return to the ancient, pre-christian system — that of the confusion of the two powers in the hands of the Temporal Ruler. But Christianity, in this its supreme condensation, the existence, outside of the Temporal Government, yet in the purely practical sphere subordinate to it, of a „kingdom" which „is *not* of this world" and whose servants therefore „do not fight" i. e. do not use temporal weapons, those of brute force, in the maintenance of the *higher law* of their „kingdom" (higher law destined finally to put an end to all fighting, to all that hideous barbarism called war) — Christianity, in this its supreme characteristic, is in no wise liable to extinction, in spite of the openly avowed hostility of the partisans of so-called modern progress, and the still more inveterate, even if unavowed, detestation of the openly and systematically retrograde partisans of the actually prevailing system of Temporal Omnipotence. It is the indestructibility of Christianity, in this its essential culmination, that makes this system so profoundly revolutionary; for it is it, at bottom, which is responsible for the whole of the actual situation. But for it, all the other difficulties, and they are many and serious, no doubt, would all be surmountable, and even, comparatively speaking, easily so.

Modern opinion will certainly every where impose, sooner or later, aided especially by the terrible lessons of experience, the condition which the modern situation, looked at as a whole, so imperatively demands, the separation of the spiritual power from the temporal power, first and foremost as this condition is among those which can alone definitively terminate the actual revolutionary state, state moreover that is constantly and surely intensified by the efforts at material compression, indispensable of course, on the part of the temporal governments, as long as we have no socially recognized, genuine and efficacious solution of the present disorder and anarchy. But the Scientific Synthesis protests energetically against the purely revolutionary measure, which, on a superficial view of the matter, may seem to be identical with the separation of the two powers, viz that commonly called the *Separation of the Church from the State*, and which conservatives would be everywhere perfectly in the right in opposing by every effectual means possible, but which unhappily they almost always do oppose by means tending infallibly to insure their own failure. For the separation of the two powers is as indispensable a measure as the revolutionary „separation of the churches from the state" is detestable and ruinous*) But

---

*) The case of England seems at first sight exceptional. The sound system of the maintenance of the Church by purely voluntary effort is there so deeply ingrained in the habits of the people, especially of those most deeply imbued with the religious spirit, that there the movement for the separation of the Church from the State is anything but irreligious in its motive. It is the very opposite indeed. The habits of the people in this regard have in fact rendered possible in England a most admirable revival there of the Mediæval Church. Still even the English „Society for the Liberation of Religion from State Control", (whose very name indicates on the part of its authors a remarkable instinctive presentiment of the true scientific conception) must just so far modify its programme as to fairly embrace the separation of the two powers, if it would completely clear its skirts of all vestige of complicity with a radically anti-christian, if not absolutely atheistic, revolutionaryism.

the revolutionary measure really means, not the so indispensable restoration of the social prestige and moral energy of the Church, certainly assured result of the sincere and honest separation of the two powers, but the speedy abolition and destruction of the Church and the consequent extirpation of religion. For it essentially consists in depriving Her of such prestige as results from Her recognition by the state, which is far from being absolutely nullified, so far as the peasantry is concerned at all events, by the slavery to the state in which She has at this day to exist, without at the same time giving Her the smallest possible compensation. As regards all the higher classes and the proletariate of the cities, the actual slavery of the Church to the State does no doubt utterly cripple, if not entirely paralyze, Her power for good, and more than any thing else — or at least with only one single exception, itself also due to the confusion of the two powers — intensify the materialistic and atheistic tendencies so unhappily prevalent, and which would alas! be only too energetic without this aid. She would gain therefore immensely by the real *separation of the two powers*, far more indeed than she would lose by the revolutionary measure. But that revolutionary measure, while depriving the Church of such prestige as State-recognition can give Her, in the actual situation so indispensable, proposes only to still further intensify the usurpation of spiritual prerogatives by the state, which is in fact the source of the greatest of all the actual dangers to the cause of Order in Europe.*)

*) The real tendencies, and indeed positively certain ultimate result, of the absolute concentration of the two powers in the hands of the Temporal Government, one can see as plainly as the sun at noon day, in Russian Nihilism, which could no doubt be developed with infallible certainty in any one of our European nations, by the simple and easy process of imitating the Russian system of Government. True, Russian Nihilism is greatly intensified by the fact, that the Russian confusion of the two powers is based still upon a theological dogma. But the Revolutionaries, or what in this connection is just the same thing, the „Liberals" of Western Europe will find, when it is too late — unless indeed a wise Conservatism steps in to reduce them to permanent impotence by substituting the true measure for the false and bastard measure — that the confusion of the two powers in the interest of materialism and practical atheism, in one word of **metaphysical Liberalism** (only a euphonious synonyme for rank Individualism and Anarchy), is even more fatally dangerous in the end to social Order than the Russian Despotism, while at the same time more radically destructive of Liberty and Human Dignity.

The true solution, by the bye, of the actual situation in the case of Russia, does not by any means consist, as it does for Western Europe, in the direct separation of the two powers, which, difficult

This digression into the very border land of concrete or practical politics, would be quite out of place here were it not that in the actual state of public opinion, and the long and practically unquestioned reign of the fatally revolutionary system of Temporal Omnipotence, the modern mind would be unable really to grasp the true significance of that fundamental condition of normal social order, the separation of

---

of realization every where, is simply impossible for Russia. Russia is very far from being included in our modern Western Civilization, and her interference in European politics properly so called, always morally a gross usurpation, is a perpetual menace to her own existence, but for which, in fact, she might after all have escaped the fearful visitation of Nihilism, a cancer in her bosom that is constantly growing. Russia is properly an Asiatic and Oriental Power, not European and Occidental. In Asia, if she can only learn in time where she has to stop, her rule is wholly beneficent, and will assure her a singularly glorious Future. But as to her European possessions, even such as are actually legitimate, her case is unique, and the true solution which it demands is destined, unless the persistent blindness of the Czars ruins her utterly, by precipitating her into a Constitutionalism totally unsuited to her situation and her magnificent possible Future, from which however nothing can save her *except* that true solution of her present most dangerous situation — to wipe out Nihilism as by a stroke of the pen, and, by a veritably magical transformation, render her, in an incredibly short space of time, the Envied among all nations, while placing her Czar among the very foremost names of all Human History.

the two powers, and indeed to form a clear and distinct conception of a true and genuine purely spiritual power, without some such concrete illustrations. But it was the service the Middle Ages rendered to the Normal Social Order of Humanity by the development of this conception, however premature may have been then its practical realization, now at last, however, positively assured (unless indeed modern society, by persisting in the revolutionary system, goes to pieces altogether) — which constitutes the chief title of this most decisive period to the eternal gratitude and reverent admiration of our Race. The inevitable result, however, of the theocratic tendencies inexpugnably inherent in any theological creed was, in the case of the admirable mediæval Catholic Church, that a struggle arose between Her and the Temporal Powers which, constantly maintained now for six centuries, has resulted in the complete subordination, not to say absolute slavery, of the Church, to the various Temporal Governments, even in the countries that remain most completely Catholic: a subordination accomplished therefore essentially in great part by Catholics themselves, and in which Catholics so eminent for their piety as to have been subsequently sainted, as in the case of St. Louis of France, have taken an eminent part. When one reflects upon the infinite blessings that would have flowed out upon all mankind had it only been possible for the eternally glorious Church of a St. Augustine and a Hildebrand, a St. Bernard and an Innocent III, a St. Francis of Assisi and a St. Elizabeth of Hungary, to have gone on unchecked in Her beneficent career, it is impossible not to regret profoundly that, in fact, the development of modern society had to be accompanied, inevitably, by a constant and progressive decay of that Church. Not but what Modern Society, when it shall at last have accomplished its destiny: the inauguration of the Normal State of Man upon the Earth, will have been well worth all it will have cost; but how fearful has been that cost! On one side five centuries of utterly useless, more and more bloody and barbarous Wars, becoming finally veritable orgies of fiends! On the other hand the Terrible Spectre of modern Revolution, now actually looming up into ever more and more hideous proportions, laughing, with its ghastly grin, at all the vain efforts of merely material and physical compression, as though to demonstrate, beyond the last possible vestige of doubt, the radical impotence of merely temporal instrumentalities in the spiritual sphere! And who knows how long the actual transitionary state, so full of dangers, as well as countless miseries, may not have yet to last!

But a Spiritual Power to be able to maintain itself in Modern Society must be perfectly pure. It must possess weapons and instrumentalities of a purely spiritual character, having native force and energy enough to enable it to dispense with any sort of aid from the Temporal Arm. Nay, it must utterly repudiate for itself all such aid, and refuse categorically the smallest vestige of any sanction, on its part, to any interference whatever of that temporal arm, in any direction, within the spiritual sphere. It must have so full and undoubting a confidence, based moreover upon experience acquired, in its own purely spiritual means and instrumentalities, as to inspire it to ask of the Temporal Government, nothing whatever but a perfectly fair and free field for their exercise. On this condition alone, can a church be entirely set free from the last tincture of theocratic aspiration, and so guaranteed, by her own character and principles, against that deplorable conflict with the Temporal Power which, more than any thing else, save only the closely allied tendency to the absorption of material wealth, certainly far more even than the merely theoretical undermining of Her dogma, put the noble and venerable Catholic Church, unhappily, into irrevocable conflict with Modern Opinion.

But the failure of the grand and glorious enterprize of the mediæval Church, which at one time seemed so very near to the definitive solution of the supreme problem of the Human Unity, was by no means due exclusively to the faults and defects of that eternally venerable Church, whom all true Positivists sincerely revere and love, in the midst of all Her sad decay. The persistence of the Catholic Church even to this day, in spite of the so profound discredit cast upon her dogma, is, on the contrary, a decisive proof of the impossibility of either setting aside the problem unsolved, leaving it to rest for ever in its actual state, without any solution at all, and an equally decisive proof of the impossibility of finding any other solution than the reorganization of a purely spiritual power, on a basis fairly irrefragable, and capable, therefore, of universal extension, thus rendering finally possible, and therefore definitively assuring, the complete separation and profound mutual independence of the two powers. But Feudalism, although it had spontaneously transformed military activity from conquering to defensive, was still an essentially military social state, and no essentially military state is compatible with a radical separation between the two powers. No Ruler whose power is based upon militarism is willing, if he can help it, to tolerate the existence of an independent church. A Priest who may invite him to moralize his own action, supremely as the corresponding society may need such moralization, will necessarily be distasteful to him. All military action tends so profoundly to develope the love of arbitrary power in the chiefs, and to habituate the people themselves to its exercise, that no military Government will ever be willing, or even able, to tolerate a Church that is not, by one means or another, in more or less absolute slavery to itself. The frank and systematic recognition of the principle of the separation of the two powers, and the definitive abandonment of the barbarous system of militarism (system certainly barbarous relatively to our modern occidental civilization, in which its action is necessarily at one and the same time retrograde and revolutionary), must needs be so essentially simultaneous as to be virtually a one act. For the whole system of militarism is in such utter antagonism to all the best and noblest tendencies of the modern spirit, as well as to the whole of the spirit and tendencies of Christianity, that it could not possibly subsist a fortnight, in the presence of a real freedom of discussion. The cause of civil and religious liberty, and that of the separation and mutual independence of the two powers, are in fact absolutely identical. It is ignorance of this fact, or what is the same thing of the true meaning of the word „liberty", that is one of the greatest dangers, perhaps the chief danger, to European peace at this day, and the incessant irritant of our revolutionary state. For the true Human Liberty is not the liberty of tigers and gorillas, the absence of all rule, of all systematic regulation. The very contrary, indeed. The true Human Liberty never exists till it is systematically instituted. What exists spontaneously is quite another thing, any thing indeed but this. Genuine, real liberty is certainly not merely the absence of a dominating Power which, simply because it is power, that is to say brute force, because therefore it *can* impose itself, pretends to be supreme judge of every thing, to decide every thing, what is true and what is false, what is right and what is wrong, to decide what people may say or write or print, and what they may not say or write or print, that pretends, or at least that would fain pretend, to decide what people shall think and what they shall not think. Were the question put in an abstract shape to any one of the five great peoples that constitute our modern Western Civilization, the properly European civilization, it would certainly prove to be the practically unanimous conviction of that people, that such a Government would constitute the complete negation of the most elementary Freedom, a Freedom universally recognized at this day as just and necessary. That, however, which gives to the actual revolutionary agitation its violence and its danger, is, that it is not understood, and especially not clearly enough understood, that the mere overthrow, overthrow by violence, of such a Government even as that just indicated, would of itself do little or nothing to insure a real Liberty. For it is a positivist maxim — and that is the same as to say a demonstrable and rationally undeniable principle — that *no Society exists without Government*. But as, on the other hand, no Government can exist without a sufficient foundation in public opinion, where there is a state of opinion such as to permit of the existence of a radically despotic government, systematic negation of all rational liberty, of all true human dignity, where for instance the people prefer not to have the trouble and responsibility of thinking for themselves, the only real remedy is in the modification of opinion, and the awakening of the public conscience to a more dignified attitude. Where there exists a sufficiently free discussion, such modifications of opinion as are really necessary naturally come about, if not quite spontaneously, at least so gradually as not to involve the smallest shock, and moreover without any injustice towards vested interests, even those that depend on the abuses to be modified. But where there is no provision for the peaceful and orderly and therefore free development of opinion, the really inevitable modifications must needs come about with more or less suddenness, the efforts to prevent them tending in fact, and at last tending irresistibly, to produce a violent explosion. It is certainly not an energetic Temporal Dictatorship that is necessarily dangerous either to liberty, to order or to progress. The Great Frederick the Second, true type, according to the positive doctrine, of Modern Polity, abundantly proved that. An energetic dictatorship, in the hands of a Ruler morally and intellectually eminent enough to be capable of profoundly respecting the separation of the two powers, that is to say of protecting a radical freedom of discussion (two things if not absolutely identical necessarily implying each other), would be, in the midst of the modern spiritual anarchy, in every respect the best and the most progressive government, the most really favorable to the true Human Liberty as well as the best guarantee of social order. But there is no reliable security whatever for Order, where there is not systematic protection for rational liberty, and profound respect for Human Dignity, both implied in and both absolutely demanding the systematic acceptance of the principle of the separation of the spiritual power from the temporal power. Anarchical Doctrines are inherently suicidal, alike in the political sphere and in the moral sphere, never so absolutely certain to break down, however contradictory the expression may seem to be, as just when they are to all appearance in the very act of succeeding triumphantly. Where, moreover, that complete negation of all rational, all properly Human Liberty and Human Dignity, the concentration of the two powers in the hands of the temporal government, actually exists, and with the real concurrence of the people, the situation will not be mended in the least by the infusion of no matter how large a dose of Democratic Institutions. So far as true liberty and human dignity are concerned, it would not mend the matter, nay, it would make it worse, for the usurping temporal government to be based entirely on democratic institutions. For practically that would necessarily mean simply the unlimited and totally irresponsible sway of the Plutocracy.

True Liberty, the veritably Human Liberty, requires, in fact,[1] to sum up in few words this most indispensable theory, basis of all genuine Social Order and still more of all profound and dignified

Moral Order, the free action of a government in harmony with the social situation, whose power is correlative to the social function it fulfils. A practical power corresponding to, and efficiently directing, the real and actual practical activity; a theoretical authority in harmony with the real beliefs of the people, capable therefore of developing in the public mind and heart, a high and ever higher moral ideal, rendering impossible the fatal scandal, repeated more than once during the last forty centuries, of setting up on the social summits an unutterable moral baseness, and treating at the same time all the noblest human aspirations, indeed all that is really virtuous, dignified, patriotic and honest in the corresponding society, not merely as dangerous but as treasonable, meriting tortures and death. To witness this spectacle we do not, unhappily, have to go back even to the days of the Christian martyrs, to the times of the Caligulas and the Neros. The spiritual power must act, moreover, exclusively by means really appropriate to the development of solid intellectual convictions, and the highest moral sentiments. The smallest imaginable employment of brute force in the sphere of Religion, and especially by or on behalf of the Priesthood itself, is even more fatal to morality and social order, to human dignity and therefore to all real human virtue, than the usurpation of spiritual functions by the temporal government.*)

*) There is yet another explanation indispensable at this point, in order to the complete appreciation of this grand principle of the separation of the two powers, the systematic development of which is incomparably the greatest service ever rendered to mankind by Positive Science. While the normal spiritual power expounds sociological science, the grand general principles underlying the social existence and the spontaneous progress of our race, and therefore indicates the lines of direction which a wise statesmanship must needs follow, furnishing that statesmanship with the abstract principles so to speak of its art, it does **not in the least degree pretend to indicate the immediate measures** appropriate to any particular situation. It recognizes the exclusive competency of the practical statesman in regard to all questions of practical application in the political sphere proper, even of the principles which sociological science has ever so fully demonstrated. The supremely dominant question in practical politics is always that of *opportunity*, and on that it does not pretend to have any competency at all. According to the scientific synthesis all questions of practical politics are in the exclusive competence, as also the exclusive responsibility, of the practical statesman; so that if this statesman decides that, in the country the political direction of which is in his hands, the time has not come for permitting the public exposition of the scientific synthesis, the competent positivist theorician will certainly not breathe the faintest whisper of protest. Even on points decided by the practical statesman in direct opposition to counsels he has offered in the name of science, the positivist theorician

But the Middle Ages prepared for the normal state of man upon the earth still more decisively yet by the admirable moral culture which the Catholic Church actually did institute, moral culture, however, essentially impossible without the separation of the two powers and the suf-

will be the first to set the example of practical submission to the practical authorities. Subsequent Experience is a judge of the wisdom or unwisdom of the proffered Counsels, whose Judgment the positivist theorician would be very ill-advised indeed to wish to forestal. Those are just the judgments, on the contrary, on which the future Spiritual Power and universal prevalence of the Positive System will almost wholly depend. It is just such judgments that have to stamp the positive synthesis as genuine science, if indeed it be such.

For the sociological theorician to interfere in the sphere of practical politics would be as absurd as for the astronomer to undertake, on the ground of his knowledge of astronomy, to set aside the experienced sea-captain and navigate the ship himself. A statesman who rejected the counsels and ignored the science of the positive sociologist would resemble simply the experienced sea-captain who, in the earliest days of modern science, declined the use of the new-fangled nautical-almanac and celestial maps, and preferred to trust simply to his empirically acquired skill. The honest Sea-Captain would have ten chances to one of coming safely into port, while the presumptuous Astronomer would certainly go to swift shipwreck, or be saved from shipwreck only by still more promptly foundering in the open sea.

Meantime the difficulties that beset the practical statesman, in the fulfilment of his so indispensable function, are at this day so great, and so constantly increasing, that it is the invariable duty of every well-instructed mind, to do every thing ficient independence of the spiritual power. In spite of a dogma altogether unsuited to the end, giving rise to obstacles and hindrances of all sorts, the Catholic Priesthood, with an admirable empirical wisdom, developed especially in the various Religious Orders, that arose from time in its power to diminish, never any thing to add to them. The accomplishment of the spontaneous progress is, in reality, so much better assured than are the supremely fundamental needs of Order, in the actual situation of to-day, that the wise policy is that which seeks before all things stability, and would fain make the inevitable modifications as gradual as possible, avoiding simply the blind resistance which renders violent explosion inevitable. And as to the positivist propagande, it ought to be introduced and encouraged only there where it will tend, and so far as it will tend, to the pacification of the public mind, in a word to the maintenance of tranquillity, object of supreme importance to-day, or on the other hand, to pave the way for modifications foreseen to be finally inevitable, and so, in both cases alike, to lighten the task of the Temporal Ruler. For the Governing Classes themselves, however, a knowledge of sociological science may have an importance of the gravest character even forthwith. It is, however, only among the central population of the Occident, whose Initiative in the grand movement of the Progress of Civilization nothing can annul, initiative at this day indeed more manifest than at any former period, that the Positivist Propagande (save only so far as the religious side of it is concerned, as the satisfaction of a purely personal moral need among a very limited class, and as a calming, pacifying influence among a class very much wider) is not only fully opportune, but of urgent necessity, even among the whole mass of the people, in the great cities especially. It must be manifest to every well-informed mind that, however urgently important to time to accomplish reforms rendered indispensable by the incurable vices of the dogma, effected a culture and development of the nobler sentiments of our common human nature, that challenges still the enthusiastic admiration of every soul in any wise capable of appreciating them. This moral culture, greatly aided by the noble institution of Chivalry, and its so characteristic worship of the Virgin Mother, was time and again defeated, relatively to the clergy itself especially, by the theocratic aspirations and corrupting temporal ambitions engendered by the dogma in the chiefs of the secular priesthood, but most of all by that inexhaustible source of corruption and demoralization for any clergy, its material wealth, the development of which the strikingly severe denunciations of the Christian scriptures could not prevent, but which suffices, even alone, to render utterly inevitable the decay and moral paralysis into which this grand and venerable Catholic Church has fallen at this day. Nothing can efficiently

---

for the peace, good order and prosperity of all Europe, may be the Inauguration of the Positive Worship of Humanity, that Worship can by no possibility be inaugurated any where outside of the City of Paris, irrevocably the universal Metropolis of Humanity.

protect any Priesthood whatever from this utterly fatal source of decay, (far more practically decisive even than the theoretical undermining of the dogma), except the systematic prevalence of the principle of the separation of the two powers, which, pushed to its just and logical ultimate result, effectually debars the priesthood from the possession of any material wealth whatsoever, even from the legal ownership of its own Temples and Schools and its own sacerdotal residences.

The double fact on which, according to Positive Science all religious Culture really depends, is, first, the general biological law that all living organs develope by exercise while they tend towards atrophy by inaction; and secondly that the expression of benevolent sentiments and of the disinterested sympathies constitutes just such an exercise, and one that is constantly optional. That any such basis for religious exercises was inconceivable, and so remains moreover, under a theological dogma, does not alter the fact, nor render any the less real the admirable results obtained by religious exercises in the long past, although instituted under the fostering guidance of theological ideas, then so natural to man, results in fact due to the above biological natural law. Nothing is to-day more important than that the modern mind, however bent it may be upon emancipating itself from theological beliefs, should learn to appreciate the magnificent results attained by the Middle Ages in this sphere of moral culture, and cease to confound the moral culture itself with the fables upon which it was in the past dogmatically based, and then inevitably so. Our supreme need is to get back, at all events, the moral culture, however different may be the dogmatic foundation on which in the future it will have to repose. The very foundation of a rational appreciation of the actual social situation, consists in a more just view than commonly prevails of this so decisive period, the Middle Ages, resplendent as it is with moral and religious glory. For thus only can be restored that historic sentiment without which all real social Order, and at least equally all real social Progress, are eternally impossible. There can in fact be no reliable progress until the *conception* of Progress is systematically linked with that of Order. That again can result only from the demonstration of the Present as the natural product of the Past, the anti-historic spirit of recent centuries being the negation of the very progress about which so many empty boasts are being made and so much unmitigated cant uttered. For the only Future really possible is that which results from the prolongation of the same lines of development as are revealed by the Past of onr Race, regarded as leading up naturally to the Present; while the competent study of that Past, from this point of view, necessarily results in a veritable demonstration of the Human Future upon the Earth, and so puts a decisive end to all sorts of disordered dreams, while giving fullest satisfaction to all sane aspirations.

To fully appreciate, however, the sublime phenomena presented to us by this truly heroic period of religion and morality, we must attentively consider the practical result that had invariably followed from the confusion of the two powers under the ancient Theocracies, confusion then no doubt inevitable, neither the theological dogma, nor a purely military temporal government, being consistent with their real and sincere separation and necessary mutual independence.

The Theocracies, even the pure theocracies under the Conservative Polytheism, always tended finally to the subordination of the priesthood to the military caste. We see the same again under the Mosaic or monotheistic Theocracy. To punish His own chosen people for their repeated rebellion against Him, God gave them a King: that was, naturally enough, the way in which the Hebrew Theocracy recorded its own defeat. According to the theological conception, King and priest was each alike the representative of the supreme God or Gods; while moreover the very Ideal of the theological theory is the unlimited sway of personal caprice. Under the scientific conception, Righteousness is regarded as necessarily in accordance with the Will of God *because it is Righteousness:* under the theological conception, Righteousness, and sometimes also the most revolting Unrighteousness, have to be regarded as Righteousness because they are declared to be *in accordance with the will of God*, an accordance, however, utterly indemonstrable. And so when, finally, the ideal moral perfection, the Infinite Goodness, became the supreme attribute of the Deity, and the *fear of God*, which was, according to the ancient Prophet the *beginning of wisdom*, began to transform itself into a filial love destined to *cast out the fear*, the anthropomorphic modification was so decisive as already to presage the advent of the one definitive conception of Humanity. But the Warrior was a so much better representative of the unlimited sway of purely personal caprice than the Priest, who was always seeking, as far as the existing conditions of positive knowledge would permit, for an Ideal Perfection, that the King always finally won, in spite of all the efforts of systematic Wisdom, his supremacy over the Pontiff. It was under Catholicism only, that the Normal Order could give a first distinct intimation of its fundamental characteristic. The complete confusion of the two powers, which is the very ideal of Monarchy in the sociological sense of this term, had always brought about so intense a concentration of Wealth and Power that a profound corruption was generated in he very heart of the social body, corruption which necessarily resulted, as all moral corruption must do when sufficiently developed, in social death. In this abyss, inevitable under such conditions, perished one after another of the ancient Theocracies, Egyptian,

Assyrian, Babylonian, and we know not how many more still earlier which have left not even a name behind them. It was only the Moslem regeneration which preserved the Hindoo civilization from total disruption. While in our modern Occidental Civilization, since the decisive triumph of the system of temporal omnipotence, relatively to our modern post-christian civilization so profoundly revolutionary, it is the resurrection of the Sardanapalian Ideal, of the Getting the Having and the Enjoying, which, in so profound harmony with the spontaneously predominant energy of our egotist and animal instincts, is at bottom the supreme danger now menacing our very existence. For in reality Human Society is based upon the gradually developing predominance of the social sympathies over the egotist and animal instincts. The vital Principle of society is **Love**: and the notable scheme of our modern „Liberalism" — which word is only a euphonic veil for an enervating and desolating Individualism — scheme for dispensing with this vital principle of all Religion and of all really human Moral Existence, and therefore of all Society in any wise capable of endurance, and substituting in its place an ingeniously contrived ponderation of material interests, is doomed to a radical and richly deserved failure. The sooner this fact is distinctly apprehended and fully understood the better for us all, and especially for those on whom the social and political responsibility rests, for our governing classes. No doubt the Church, both in its ancient trunk and in its modern offshoots, does perfectly understand it already. But with its hands and feet in irons, what can it do? It is to knock off those fetters and those manacles (including the self-imposed — perhaps especially these) that is the supremely important aim to-day, one that, with a little serious and unprejudiced meditation, must necessarily command the energetic concurrence of every really thoughtful mind; aim to which at all events all the Positivist Religious Propagande ought to be systematically subordinated.

The institution of a morality independent of and superior to mere legality, which, presaged as in fact it had been many centuries earlier, was the fundamental characteristic of Christianity, and the practical development of which, and in a manner supremely admirable, was the greatest service of all accomplished on behalf of our Race by the mediæval civilization rendered possible a most energetic reaction against this ever-besetting, but worse than bestial Sardanapalian Ideal: the brutes fulfil their destiny, but man, in persisting in a career of sensuality and selfishness, tramples his into the mire and mud. The fundamental constitution of our individual nature, however, renders this ideal, worse than bestial though it be, our eternally besetting danger; for if the egotist and animal instincts had not a very decisive predominance of spontaneous energy over the social sympathies, there would be wanting, especially in the absence of any systematic conception of our real nature and destiny, the indispensable guarantee for the conservation of our personal existence; without which conservation nevertheless, society itself must come to an end But without a powerful reaction against the spontaneously dominant egotism, society equally perishes, although from an opposite tendency, that towards sensual corruption. It was just this element in the teachings of the Nazarenes, that commended this sect to the great St. Paul, when he spontaneously felt the need of some new regenerative influence in the Greco-Roman

World, to counteract the degrading moral tendencies of the Greek civilization, and at the same time saw plainly, that a monotheistic basis was indispensable for any influence that could then be sufficiently energetic. In the teachings of Jesus, the hostility to material accumulations was radical and absolute: the rich man was, as such, profoundly at enmity with God; he must part with all his individual wealth, and bring every thing into the common treasury of the family of the saints, as the fundamental condition of his admission into the Kingdom of God, which was to be forthwith established upon the Earth The radically communist character of the Gospels, and the other Christian sacred Books, abundantly justified the wise precaution of the Catholic Church, in withholding them from the undirected study and comments of the laity. Not because there would be any danger of the Communist Ideal's having any widespread practical prevalence. The system of a common ownership of all material possessions, beyond articles of strictly personal use, served an inestimable purpose, an end of incalculably high social value, in the case of the monastic institutions, during the development of the Feudo-

Catholic civilization, however intolerable the abuses those institutions may have afterwards developed; and even now, within certain limited spheres of the kind, that system may not be without its use. But that system is conciliable only with a very pristine stage of social development, as the basis of the common social life. A people subjected to a crushing despotism, which utterly debars them from participation in any larger social life, may find in such a system a certain material defence, and even a narrowly limited play for the social sentiments. But, save in some such conditions, it is utterly inadmissible. Radically inconsistent with every kind of progress, because radically irreconcileable with any kind of freedom, it deprives life of all stimulus, and tends towards an utterly unendurable *ennui*. All attempts to artificially institute such a system, made under a regime of social and political liberty that gives free play to such experiments, utterly break down after a very short experience. The same system imposed by force, as it could be only by a political surprise, would quite certainly come to the same end, only more speedily, making the experiment, as an experiment, worthless. No doubt the actual state of our modern European or Western Civilization, does expose us to this, and all sorts of other surprises. But that which was at stake in the early days of Christianity, was the moral culture capable of being evoked from the Nazarene teaching, and all the rest of that admirable Feudo-catholic civilization we are this day contemplating.

This Catholic moral culture, however, was also in its turn directed — as indeed all moralities, properly so-called, all above the most elementary (or rather the merely spontaneous, due simply to the bare fact of social existence), have necessarily had to be — against the same danger, essentially consisting, in fact, in the unchecked domination in our individual life of the nutritive instinct and the sexual instinct, the two lowest of our egotist and animal instincts, and therefore by far the most energetic. These two, among the seven impulsions which constitute the lower side of our individual nature, are spontaneously so much the most energetic, that the whole question of the moral regeneration and purification of that nature, and therefore of the development of the normal social harmony, depends on the surmounting of the immense spontaneous predominance of these two closely allied, although often practically divergent, instincts. The triumphant success of the mediæval church, in both regards, was something unspeakably admirable, especially in view of the utter want of adaptation in the dogma to the end that needed attainment, and that was in fact to so eminent a degree attained. There is no shadow of ground for imagining the mediæval moral culture destined to any ultimate failure, or for supposing any such failure in any wise possible, had it been instituted on the dogmatic basis of conceptions capable of retaining their hold upon men's beliefs. In relation to both these instincts, on the contrary, the successes attained were most decisive, and indeed glorious.

What phenomena have ever been developed in human society, that can surpass in sublimity those obtained by the Catholic Church, in the twelfth and thirteenth centuries, in repression of the nutritive instinct? All the circumstances and social conditions favored the worst abuses. Manners were rough and uncultured, unless in the returning Crusaders, already corrupted, and with faith broken down. And yet we see the Clarisses and the third Order of St. Francis, drawing into their ranks the sons and daughters of monarchs and reigning dukes, and developing far and wide, among the great and the mighty and the wealthy, a veritable passion for poverty. And in regard to the sexual instinct, the triumph was even more decisive still, as being still more difficult to obtain. It was among the great and and the mighty, also, that were developed those very remarkable chaste marriages, that might have grown, with due systematic encouragement, into a grand and permanent institution, with incalculably beneficent results, under the unspeakably admirable Worship of the Virgin Mother, so greatly fostered by, and so immensely aiding to develope and to ennoble, the Institution of Chivalry. Of course the specific practical results were marred by the absolute spirit of theologism, which at every point tends to defeat the moral culture, first poisoning its very foundation principle and then perverting its practical reactions.*)

---

*) The incurable tendency of Theological Dogma, becoming only intensified in this its period of decay, to betray and finally sacrifice the Religion built up on its foundation, is remarkably manifested, both as to kind and degree, among the Protestant Sects. The so-called Reformation brought about, no doubt, a certain recrudescence of theologism, ultimating now-a-days in some curious phenomena, especially in the development of a fetichistic worship of the Bible, which, as so much paper,

But the immense success of the Culture as such remains beyond all possible challenge or doubt, eternal source of highest hopes for the Human Future. The moral culture is, in reality, simply a natural development, although needing to be made systematic; development

printed in a certain fashion, and in a peculiar style of calf-binding, constitutes, especially in the United States of America, a sort of Idol, whose worship is not one whit more elevating than that of the metallic Idols furnished by the Christian manufacturers of the English Town of Birmingham, and the Christian merchants of English seaports, to our fellowmen in the more backward stages of social development, furnished, too, along with whiskey and other worse and more deadly poisons that cannot even be named, (some Bibles being of course thrown in), at the cannon's mouth, in the name of „Progress" and „Civilization". But as to the contents of the same Bible, in the more and more rare cases in which it is actually read, its communistic and other moral tendencies are completely neutralized by a process of pretended spiritualization, the honest name of which is simply mystification, and which process does really, to use the biblical phraseology, „make the word of God of none effect by the traditions" of the theologians. This mode also of utterly sacrificing Christian Religion to a professedly Christian Dogma, needs also to be brought to a complete and immediate end, if our modern society is not to perish incontinently in a slough of unfathomable corruption, which Newspaper exposures and parliamentary or other *Commissions of Inquiry* can do nothing to cure, but may easily make worse, by putting the Public Conscience on a wrong scent, especially in leading it to trust to legal remedies, necessarily altogether illusory, and so diverting it from the only real remedy, the indispensably necessary rejuvenation of Religion.

of the higher side of our nature relatively to
the lower — development of the noble spirit
of self-sacrifice, spirit which still furnishes
triumphant manifestations, most unmistakeable,
of the fact that it cannot die out from among
men, whatever may become of the theological
beliefs with which the culture of that spirit was
formerly linked. The question is being forced,
now, upon the attention of the thoughtful and
conscientious, within quite as much as without
the pale of the Christian Churches, Catholic
and Protestant, whether it be really the fact
that theological beliefs have become, at last,
directly hostile to the development of this truly
divine spirit, which six centuries ago was so
admirably developed under their banner. It depends upon the attitude which the Heads and
Leaders of the Christian Churches henceforth
take, under the so entirely altered relations
between Science and Religion, what answer the
really thoughtful, conscientious and sincere will
finally have to make to this question.

In order to direct the actual conduct under
the impulsion of this noble and truly divine
spirit, positive science, Sociological Science, is
no doubt necessary; it alone indicates with

sufficient exactitude the normal state of man upon the Earth, objective aim of all wise devotedness. Still more is sociological science exclusively competent to indicate the means by which ends, ever so universally desired and longed for by a highly developed moral sense and genuine Christian sentiment, can be securely and peacefully attained, without shock, material or moral, and without economical derangement. But it is only the atheistic Specialist Science and the pure Quackeries that under the specialist regime can so easily impose themselves on the modern mind, committing fearful ravages — the „Modern Science" in whose adulterous embraces the Church is forced, in Her actual alliance with the State, to live, to the ruin of Her own moral energy and Her efficacy on behalf of social order, — that has ever dared, in its sacrilegious irruptions into this sacred sphere. to propound theories, like those of the Political Economists for instance, in open defiance of the most fundamental principles of Christian Morality. But so magical and irresistible a power is wielded at this day by Positive Science, that a pure quackery. that has nothing of science about it but its bare name, and that an impudent usurpation, was able, for a whole generation and more, to strike dumb the Christian Churches by the mere terror of its usurped name, no one daring to utter a whisper of protest against its rank and blasphemous atheisms. The Scientific Synthesis, on the contrary, is in so profound harmony with all the Christian Ideal, that there are but few elements indeed in the Positive Regime, or system of practical life logically resulting from the sociological theories, which might not, with the utmost consistency, and with scarcely more than a shadow of modification, be adopted by any Christian Church, and enforced by the precepts of its own dogma upon its disciples and adherents. Nay, one cannot be really faithful to the Gospel Teachings, really faithful to the glorious traditions of the Mediæval Church, without thus more or less appropriating the positive regime. Certainly no enlightened Christian would, in this nineteenth century, dissipate the material treasures entrusted by the Divine Providence (or by Humanity) to his keeping and administration, (the essential fact remains, unchanged by differences in our human phraseology), treasures whose social efficacy demands at once a high degree of concentration and a strictly individual appropriation, either on his own frivolous amusement, to say nothing of sensual indulgences which to the true Christian, as much as to the religious Positivist, are a scorn and an abomination, nor on the other hand in an unwise improvident, and insulting so-called charity, that every one knows now to have no other result, than the still further impoverishment and moral degradation of the poor. The intelligent Christian, at the end of this nineteenth century, in recognizing himself as simply the steward of his Lord and Saviour in respect to his material wealth, just as much as the Positivist in recognizing himself directly and frankly as the steward of Humanity, will so administer his wealth as to tend, in the highest degree, to Social and Moral Order and Harmony, and thus indirectly to the highest well-being of the whole Human Race. Nor certainly would that same intelligent Christian, if perchance he could come to appreciate the unspeakable blessedness, and profoundly ennobling reactions, of the habit of permanent and systematic chastity in the conjugal relation, (or what is the same thing, to understand the inevitably and profoundly degrading tendency of all sexual indulgence for its own sake) — suffer that wise and intelligent appreciation to deprive domestic life of its chief ornament, its highest joy, and its supreme social end, in the rearing of a wisely restricted number of children, assuring thus, at once the perpetuation and also the ever-upward development of our Human Race. It is, on the contrary, by a wise and efficient regulation of domestic life — that sacred sphere into which the rude and profane hands of temporal authority can never penetrate without desecrating it — that a renewed moral culture, finally, it may be hoped, to become even far more efficient, more lofty, more profoundly searching, than that of the eternally glorious Mediæval Church, (at this day, save in very narrow and exceptional spheres, so deplorably forgotten and abandoned), will most effectually of all aid in terminating the actual social disorders, quench the revolutionary spirit, by diverting into other channels all that element of it which consists of really sane aspirations, (and without which element it would soon die out of itself), and so most efficiently of all prepare for that Kingdom of God which the scientific synthesis designates the **Normal State of Man upon the Earth.**

This is the fundamental significance of the

retention, by the Positive Religion of Humanity, of the gracious and benign figure of the Virgin-Mother as an object of very special adoration. The last vestige of superstitious fable being dropped from this conception, as from the other sublime, eternal realities of Christianity, it remains purely a noble ideal, a chivalrous aspiration, an extreme, utopian limit to a profoundly real, sublime, eternal progress, traceable downwards to the very lowest animal and vegetable organism in the grand Universal Biological Hierarchy, progress, relatively to the human race, away from a worse than bestial carnality, up towards a perfectly pure and holy love, the only love truly and distinctively human, the only love that, among genuinely cultured souls, really deserves the name of love, the love that asks only to devote itself freely to its object, profoundly appreciating the truth, inaccessible to the coarse, materialistic natures, that in periods of social decay become so numerous — that *it is more blessed to love than to be loved*. In the positivist religious propagande this conception naturally takes a prominent, indeed a supreme place, the gracious figure of the Virgin-Mother, with Her child in Her arms or at Her knees, being recognized as the true visual Representative of Humanity; but here, in these annual lectures, just as in the systematic Public Instruction instituted in the actual situation by the Positive School, all that is appropriate is simply to indicate the fact that positive moral science, the real, the genuine science which teaches the immutable natural laws of our individual human nature, does in fact culminate in just this Ideal. But, for many and various reasons, too obvious to need explicit mention, it is clearly manifest that, in these purely scientific and philosophical Expositions, it would be quite out of place to expatiate upon a topic, so directly and almost exclusively appealing to the highest and noblest sentiments of the Human Heart.

III.

But the definitive advent of a systematically peaceful social activity in the temporal sphere, and in the spiritual of a complete system of conceptions all purely demonstrable, rendering for the first time fully possible a truly Universal Religion, and rendering therefore its appearance among us sooner or later fully certain, and with a universal religion, a fully planetary priesthood, is the grand phenomenon presented by the last six centuries, side by side with the sad spectacle of the long, painful, more and more disorderly decay of the mediæval system. It is this double movement of decomposition and of recomposition, which we shall have to study together next year. If, in fact, circumstances permit of our meeting together again, on the next recurrence of this anniversary, we shall have to review the services rendered by Auguste Comte in the elucidation of that grand, and yet in many respects gloomy, Historic Period, the **Development of Modern Society**, stretching from the middle of the thirteenth to the end of the eighteenth centuries. Then the year following, if nothing occur to render the continuation of these Annual Lectures impossible or undesirable, we shall study the Theory developed by the same unexampled Thinker in regard to **the Great Modern Crisis**, which, rendered inevitable by the immense difficulty of the double transition that then had to be effected, broke out in France in 1789, and, in spite of the peculiar circumstances which there imparted to it a special intensity, making it seem for the moment to be a phenomenon exclusively French, soon made manifest its essential character, as common in its fundamental conditions to all the five Great Peoples included in our Modern Occidental Civilization. This difficult transition, as long as it remains merely spontaneous, as indeed it must needs do until it be fairly understood, necessarily keeps our Modern Society in a state of revolutionary fermentation, only too full of danger, a state that will entirely cease, as soon as the transition can be transformed from spontaneous to systematic, by the advent of a sufficient knowledge of the transition that will, in any case, have to get itself effectuated.

Nothing is more important for the peace and good order of Society, than that the changes, which become, in fact, inevitable, should not be left to be brought about by revolutionary struggles from below, but should, on the contrary, be accomplished in a calm, peaceful, gradual and orderly manner from above, by the action of the enlightened Statesman. If only Louis XVI had stood faithfully by his Heaven-sent Minister, the great and wise Turgot, the violent struggles of 1789 had been unnecessary, and therefore could never have happened. And it was his own better self, too, to which the unhappy Louis was unfaithful, as well as to his immortal Minister, when, in an ill-fated hour in the year 1776, he consented to the fatal dismissal, that was fraught with so unhappy consequences for the whole of our modern Europe. But the blind struggle with the nascent new order of things, into which Louis XVI was enticed, even after 1789, struggle that cost him and so many others their lives, is a striking proof of the danger of leaving the inevitable modifications to be forced on society from below. For when the natural Leaders of Society themselves undertake the accomplishment of these modifications, that accomplishment in no wise necessitates any abrupt or perturbating changes in the *personnel* of Government, or any dangerous interference with existing interests. The inevitable transformation consists essentially only in this very simple fact, that there is a new kind of activity that, by the aid of new methods, needs direction: if violent changes occur in the *personnel* of the Governing Classes, it is simply because these older classes are unable or unwilling to undertake the new Functions. But the violence and painfulness of all the modifications really necessary, may be entirely saved, where the nature of the inevitable transition is sufficiently known to permit the accomplishment of the transition to be effected under the practical direction of the natural chiefs of the body politic, through the instrumentality of an accomplished Statesman enlightened by Positive Science. If there be any difficulty at all in the matter, it can only arise from the fact that Turgots and Leon Gambettas are not to be had for the mere asking. It remains to be seen whether they can be developed. They certainly cannot be by any system of education that altogether excludes investigation of the phenomena that have to be dealt with.

Three years from to-day, which will be the hundredth year of this great modern crisis, we shall have, supposing circumstances still to permit the continuation of these Anniversary Lectures, to dwell on the brilliant picture of the **Future State of Man upon the Earth**, deduced by Auguste Comte, with strict scientific exactitude, from the wise co-ordination of the several elements of that state spontaneously developed in the past. While in the three subsequent years, the work of Auguste Comte being then sufficiently known, at least in its most important aspect, we shall be free to direct our contemplation more specifically to the person of this unexampled Renovator, and in three successive Lectures we will consider *Auguste Comte the Philosopher*, *Auguste Comte the Founder* and *Auguste Comte the Man*. The entire Series, of Eight Lectures, will then comprize a complete and authentic account, only from a popular rather than an academical point of view, of the Life and Work of the extraordinary man, who is but now beginning to be known, and who will be truly appreciated only centuries hence. For Auguste Comte accomplished Three distinct Theoretical Constructions, each one of which would have sufficed to win for him the Immortality of an Aristotle or of a Descartes. But all this vast labor sums itself up in the decisive and irrefragable demonstration of the continuous and irresistible supremacy of Moral Considerations in the ensemble of Human Existences. This supremacy may be overlooked for a time, and indeed altogether ignored, and yet society not go all to pieces immediately. Happily it is possible for society to live, for a considerable time, on its inherited moral capital. But, with that neglect of the supreme destinies of Humanity the social decomposition begins, decomposition that nothing can arrest but a sincere repentance of the moral treason committed, repentance manifested, as sincere repentance always has to be, by an abandonment of the evil ways, and a frank and honest return to the normally supreme allegiance.

Henry Edger

Born 22 January 1820 at Chelwood Gate parish of Fletching, Sussex, England, since 18 November 1861 adoptive citizen of the United States of America: (declaration of intention filed 23 April 1851.)

Presbourg (9 Conventgasse) Hungary
24 Descartes 97 (31 October 1885.)

A paraître incessamment:

Auguste Comte et le Moyenâge:

conférence faite devant un cercle privé dans la Ville de Presbourg le samedi, 24 Guttemberg 97 (5 Septembre 1885.)

Par HENRY EDGER,

Citoyen adoptif (anglais de naissance) de l'État de New-York, États-Unis d'Amérique.

En préparation pour la Presse:

Indications simples et sommaires

quant à la

RELIGION POSITIVE DE L'HUMANITÉ.

Par le même Auteur.

A paraître plus tard:

La Prière Positive

et les autres pratiques purement personelles de la

Religion Positive de l'Humanité.

Par le même Auteur.

LA REVUE OCCIDENTALE

organe de

l'École Positiviste,

publiée sous la direction de M. Pierre Laffitte, paraît tous les deux mois. L'Abonnement par an, affranchissement compris, 20 francs, se fait chez M. Vaillant Administrateur de la Revue au Bureau, 10 Rue Monsieur-le-Prince, Paris.

By the same Author preparing for the press:
Simple and summary Indications
relative to the
Positive Religion of Humanity.

By the same Author (to appear later)
PRIVATE PRAYER
and the other purely personal practices of the
Positive Religion of Humanity.

INTERNATIONAL POLICY.
Essays
By various Authors, on the
Foreign Relations of England.
The fundamental doctrine of modern Social Life
is the subordination of politics to morals.
„AUGUSTE COMTE".

Second Edition.
London: Chapman and Hall Limited.
1884.

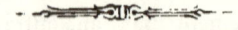

Printed by Carl Angermayer, Presbourg, Hungary.

www.ingramcontent.com/pod-product-compliance
Lightning Source LLC
Chambersburg PA
CBHW022142160426
43197CB00009B/1391